Why Do Teachers Need to Know about Psychology?

PERSONAL, SOCIAL AND EMOTIONAL PERSPECTIVES FOR EDUCATORS

Series Editor: Sue Soan, Canterbury Christ Church University, UK

Why Do Teachers Need to Know about Child Development? Strengthening Professional Identity and Well-Being, edited by Daryl Maisey and Verity Campbell-Barr

Why Do Teachers Need to Know about Diverse Learning Needs? Strengthening Professional Identity and Well-Being, edited by Sue Soan

Why Do Teachers Need to Know about Psychology? Strengthening Professional Identity and Well-Being, edited by Jeremy Monsen, Lisa Marks Woolfson and James Boyle

Other titles available from Bloomsbury

Reflective Teaching in Early Education, Jennifer Colwell and Amanda Ince with Helen Bradford, Helen Edwards, Julian Grenier, Eleanor Kitto, Eunice Lumsden, Catriona McDonald, Juliet Mickelburgh, Mary Moloney, Sheila Nutkins, Ioanna Palaiologou, Deborah Price and Rebecca Swindells

Readings for Reflective Teaching in Early Education, edited by Jennifer Colwell and Andrew Pollard

Reflective Teaching in Schools, Andrew Pollard with Pete Dudley, Steve Higgins, Kristine Black-Hawkins, Gabrielle Cliff Hodges, Mary James, Sue Swaffield, Mandy Swann, Mark Winterbottom, Mary Anne Wolpert and Holly Linklater

Readings for Reflective Teaching in Schools, edited by Andrew Pollard

Reflective Teaching in Further, Adult and Vocational Education, Margaret Gregson and Sam Duncan with Kevin Brosnan, Jay Derrick, Gary Husband, Lawrence Nixon, Trish Spedding, Rachel Stubley and Robin Webber-Jones

Reading for Reflective Teaching in Further, Adult and Vocational Education, Margaret Gregson, Lawrence Nixon, Andrew Pollard and Trish Spedding

Reflective Teaching in Higher Education, Paul Ashwin with David Boud, Susanna Calkins, Kelly Coate, Fiona Hallett, Gregory Light, Kathy Luckett, Jan McArthur, Iain McLaren, Monica McLean, Velda McCune, Katarina Mårtensson and Michelle Tooher

Why Do Teachers Need to Know about Psychology?

Strengthening Professional Identity and Well-Being

Edited by
Jeremy Monsen,
Lisa Marks Woolfson
and James Boyle

BLOOMSBURY ACADEMIC
LONDON • NEW YORK • OXFORD • NEW DELHI • SYDNEY

BLOOMSBURY ACADEMIC
Bloomsbury Publishing Plc
50 Bedford Square, London, WC1B 3DP, UK
1385 Broadway, New York, NY 10018, USA
29 Earlsfort Terrace, Dublin 2, Ireland

BLOOMSBURY, BLOOMSBURY ACADEMIC and the Diana logo are trademarks of
Bloomsbury Publishing Plc

First published in Great Britain, 2021

Copyright © Jeremy Monsen, Lisa Marks Woolfson, James Boyle and Contributors, 2021

The Editors and Contributors have asserted their right under the Copyright, Designs and Patents Act, 1988, to be identified as Author of this work.

For legal purposes the Acknowledgements on p. xviii constitute an extension of this copyright page.

Cover design by Charlotte James
Cover image © naqiewei/ iStock

All rights reserved. No part of this publication may be reproduced or transmitted in any form or by any means, electronic or mechanical, including photocopying, recording, or any information storage or retrieval system, without prior permission in writing from the publishers.

Bloomsbury Publishing Plc does not have any control over, or responsibility for, any third-party websites referred to or in this book. All internet addresses given in this book were correct at the time of going to press. The author and publisher regret any inconvenience caused if addresses have changed or sites have ceased to exist, but can accept no responsibility for any such changes.

A catalogue record for this book is available from the British Library.

Library of Congress Cataloging-in-Publication Data

Names: Monsen, Jeremy, editor. | Woolfson, Lisa Marks, editor. | Boyle, James, editor.
Title: Why Do Teachers Need to Know about Psychology?: Strengthening Professional Identity and Well-Being / Edited by Jeremy Monsen, Lisa Marks Woolfson and James Boyle.
Description: London; New York: Bloomsbury Academic, 2021. |
Series: Personal, social and emotional perspectives for educators | Includes bibliographical references and index.
Identifiers: LCCN 2020036941 (print) | LCCN 2020036942 (ebook) | ISBN 9781350084865 (hardback) | ISBN 9781350084858 (paperback) | ISBN 9781350084889 (ebook) |
ISBN 9781350084872 (epub)
Subjects: LCSH: Educational psychology. | School children--Psychology. | Teaching--Psychological aspects. | Teacher-student relationships.
Classification: LCC LB1051.W55 2021 (print) | LCC LB1051 (ebook) | DDC 370.15–dc23
LC record available at https://lccn.loc.gov/2020036941
LC ebook record available at https://lccn.loc.gov/2020036942

ISBN:	HB:	978-1-3500-8486-5
	PB:	978-1-3500-8485-8
	ePDF:	978-1-3500-8488-9
	ePUB:	978-1-3500-8487-2

Series: Personal, Social and Emotional Perspectives for Educators

Typeset by Integra Software Services Pvt. Ltd.
Printed and bound in Great Britain

To find out more about our authors and books visit www.bloomsbury.com and sign up for our newsletters.

Kneale Monsen (1928–2019)
Esta Marks (1925–2005)
Gerald Boyle (1913–91) and Catherine Boyle (1916–2012)

Contents

List of Figures ix
List of Tables x
Series Editor's Preface xi
Series Editor's Introduction to the Personal, Social and Emotional Perspectives for Educators Series xii
Using This Book xiv
About the Editors xv
About the Contributors xvi
Acknowledgements xviii
List of Abbreviations xix

1 **Setting the Context** *Jeremy Monsen, Lisa Marks Woolfson and James Boyle* 1

2 **The Professional Self and Psychology** *James Boyle, Jeremy Monsen and Lisa Marks Woolfson* 19

3 **Health and Well-Being in Psychology** *Lisa Marks Woolfson and Stuart Woodcock* 43

4 **The Social World of the Classroom** *Matthew P. Somerville and Ed Baines* 59

5 **Effective Interpersonal Communication** *Jeremy Monsen, Linda Crichton and Julie Shaw* 83

6 **Resilience, Reflection and Reflexivity** *James Boyle and Elizabeth N. King* 107

7 Psychology and the Effective Teacher *Lisa Marks Woolfson, James Boyle and Jeremy Monsen* 129

References 138
Index 158

Figures

2.1 'Roles' of a teacher: findings from a thematic analysis of job descriptions 21
4.1 Map of Ms Sua's classroom 60
5.1 Two types of theories of action (after Argyris and Schön, 1974) 94
5.2 Single- and double-loop learning. Source: Adapted from Robinson, Viviane (2018). Reduce Change to Increase Improvement. Corwin: Sage. Figure 2.4, page 21 95

Tables

1.1 Framework to guide the coaching process and relationship (GROWER model) 6
2.1 Responsibilities and illustrative examples of the role of 'Teaching' 22
2.2 Responsibilities of the 'Pastoral' role 25
2.3 Responsibilities and illustrative examples of the 'Development and Professional Training' role 26
2.4 Responsibilities and illustrative examples of the 'Working with Colleagues' role 27
2.5 Responsibilities and illustrative examples of the 'Communication' role 27
2.6 Responsibilities and illustrative examples of the 'Citizenship and Ethos' role 28
2.7 Responsibilities and illustrative examples of the 'Administration' role 28
4.1 Forms of ability grouping 64
5.1 Model I – Strategies aimed at controlling and winning 90
5.2 Accessible Dialogue – Strategies aimed at guiding more effective interpersonal problem-solving 92

Series Editor's Preface

The textbooks in the *Personal, Social and Emotional Perspective for Educators* series are explicitly designed to support teachers in establishing and developing an holistic understanding of a teacher's role and responsibilities in the twenty-first century. They specifically aim to help trainee, beginning and experienced teachers gain both confidence and knowledge in their professional role working with pupils from the early years through to university entrance. Each book asks the question '*Why do teachers need to know about …* ' and is focused on a different area of pedagogy crucial for modern-day teaching practice, providing a breadth of perspectives about teaching and learning. Importantly, in conjunction with this they provide practice examples and searching questions which challenge readers to consider their own views, beliefs and values, on child development, special, able and talented and dual exceptionality and psychology. This innovative book series gives teachers the opportunity and space to develop an enhanced understanding of their role and the professional self.

Recognizing the importance of both practice and theory every chapter is co-authored by a teacher practitioner from various stages of schooling and an education academic, enabling real-life cases from around the world to be discussed alongside theoretical and research-based studies. Although chapter titles will differ between the books, the same topics of discussion will be critically explored in most cases. These will consider the importance of the professional self, health and well-being, outdoor education, technology, listening to pupils and reflective practice.

My editorial colleagues and I hope this book series will provide you with a clear sense of the significance and value of the teacher's role and the art of inclusive teaching for all pupils. Teaching is without doubt a demanding and all-encompassing profession, but with resilience and a continuing willingness to learn and adapt, it is one of the most rewarding.

Dr Sue Soan
Series Editor

Series Editor's Introduction to the *Personal, Social and Emotional Perspectives for Educators* Series

This is a textbook trilogy which will help trainee, beginning and experienced teachers gain confidence and knowledge in working with pupils aged two through to nineteen (and perhaps even beyond). Unlike other texts it provides teachers with the opportunity to consider their practice not only from the perspective of strategies or interventions used and curricula engaged with, but also through a holistic examination of their professional role and responsibilities.

The titles of the book series *Personal, Social and Emotional Perspectives for Educators* are:

Why Do Teachers Need to Know about Child Development?
Why Do Teachers Need to Know about Diverse Learning Needs?
Why Do Teachers Need to Know about Psychology?

The series aims to enable every teacher to see why and how it is essential they recognize their own personal, social and emotional responsibilities when educating their pupils. It is for this reason the titles of each book ask a question. The editors consider it is important for all teachers to consistently ask the question 'why?' from their own personal perspective as well as from a professional perspective. Without this ongoing reflection and reflexivity, practice can become 'stale' and views 'fixed'. Twenty-first-century life is not static, but constantly changing and throwing humankind unexpected challenges, requiring professionals and leaders to be flexible, well-informed change-agents and open to new knowledge. But, of course, it is no use asking 'why?' if the 'how' and 'what' are neglected because without a focus on these types of questions as well teachers will not know what needs to change or how to change them. Thus, throughout the series, answers to the 'why?' questions are given through exploration of the 'what and how', enabling teachers the opportunity to develop a deep understanding of how they can enhance their practice and as a consequence maintain motivation and enhance their resilience and expertise.

The books are written with an international audience in mind and hope to support all teachers around the world whatever their context or pupil age group. The decision was made that the term 'pupil' would be used to try and avoid confusion between school pupils and teacher trainees or students. This generic term also facilitated avoiding the often-artificial boundaries teachers and other educators put around practice for different age groups. All children and young people, whatever their age, learning, social or emotional needs are therefore called pupils. It is hoped that no-one is offended by this decision and if so, that was not the intention. All actual names used in chapters have been altered to maintain anonymity unless specific written agreement has been obtained stating that their name or the name of an institution can be used. Of course, language has not been altered in any quotations, in the Window on research or Case studies and 'child' or 'children' is used when parental perspectives are offered.

Whichever book in the series is picked up first readers will find that all authors examine, through the subject content, what it means to be a 'teacher'. They consider not only aspects such as the professional self, but also the role of reflection and reflexivity in developing an understanding of the self and the day-to-day experiences in teaching. For clarity, *reflection* is defined in the books as the action of personal purposeful thinking about education to improve professional practice. *Reflexivity* involves 'question[ing] our own attitudes, theories-in-use, values, assumptions, prejudices and habitual actions; to understand our complex roles in relation to others' (Bolton and Delderfield, 2018:10 in Chapter 8 of *Why Do teachers Need to Know about Diverse Learning Needs?*). As Codina and Fordham (2021:120, in Soan, 2021:119–136) state 'a teacher's reflexive awareness should therefore shape their in-action reflections; i.e. the in the moment choices teachers make concerning interactions with others (colleagues, parents, children).'

Recognizing the significance of connecting theory to practice and vice versa each chapter (with the exception of chapter 1 in *Why Do Teachers Need to Know about Diverse Learning Needs?*) is co-written by a teacher practitioner and an education academic. This enables the welding together of practice experience and knowledge, and theoretical and research evidence, rather than just providing a passing glance from one arena to the other.

Finally, it is anticipated that these books will provide teachers at all stages of their professional career with the information and challenge required for them to see the significance and value of the teacher role and the art of teaching for all pupils whatever their learning or developmental needs. Humankind needs teachers now more than ever who can motivate, capture their pupils' interests and abilities, and challenge them to always ask questions and seek answers. Teaching can be without doubt the most fulfilling profession when fully understood, and it is suggested that as a natural consequence of this every pupil then becomes inclusively taught, valued and nurtured.

Dr Sue Soan
Series Editor

Using This Book

Each book follows a similar structure. Due to its professional parameters and distinctive focus, *Why Do Teachers Need to Know about Psychology?* considers technology and learning environments within chapters rather than having specific chapters on these topics. Each chapter is designed to critically explore different subject areas. These are reflected across the trilogy and are considered important to professional development today and include:

- The professional self
- Health and well-being
- The learning environment
- Technology
- Listening
- Professional relationships and collaboration
- Resilience, reflection, reflexivity
- The role of the teacher

Within each chapter

Each chapter includes a number of features to make connections between theory and practice explicit and alive, drawing on experiences and research from a range of settings:

 Case studies

 Window on research

 Window on practice
(Why do Teachers Need to Know About Child Development?)

 Reflective questions

 Reflexive questions

Each chapter ends with an Annotated bibliography.

At the end of the book

In order to also support busy educators, trainees and teachers all of the references, whilst placed together towards the end of the book, are listed in chapter order.

Editors

Jeremy J. Monsen is Principal Educational and Child Psychologist overseeing the delivery of psychological services to children and young people across two London boroughs (Westminster and Kensington & Chelsea, as part of a Bi-Borough Children's Service, UK). Jeremy is also seconded as Lecturer (Honorary) to University College, London, UK, and to the UCL Institute of Education, University College London, UK, and is Senior Research Fellow at Canterbury Christ Church University, UK. Jeremy trained as a teacher and then as an educational and child psychologist at the University of Auckland, New Zealand/Aotearoa. Jeremy undertook his PhD at UCL and his research interests cover inclusive education, classroom environment, and the development of effective applied psychological and teaching practice.

Lisa Marks Woolfson is Emeritus Professor of Psychology at the University of Strathclyde, UK, where she was Head of the School of Psychological Sciences and Health. She was Visiting Professor at Macquarie University, Australia. Lisa has been involved in the professional training of teachers, educational psychologists, and speech and language therapists. She is a registered educational psychologist with the Health and Care Professions Council.

James Boyle is Emeritus Professor of Psychology at the University of Strathclyde, UK, and was previously Honorary Professor of Education at the University of Edinburgh, UK. A local authority educational psychologist for over ten years, he is a Health and Care Professions Council Registered Psychologist and was Director of the MSc in Educational Psychology training programme at the University of Strathclyde, UK, for over twenty years. He also has experience of professional teacher education.

Contributors

Edward (Ed) Baines is Senior Lecturer in Psychology and Education at the UCL Institute of Education, University College London, UK. He has an extensive record in educational and psychological research and has a long-standing interest in teaching and learning and peer interactions and relationships in classroom settings, and in children's social lives in and outside of school. Ed currently teaches students at Undergraduate, Masters and Doctoral levels. He is Research Coordinator for the Doctorate in Educational Psychology.

Linda Crichton has worked in Education for Westminster City Council, UK, since 2002. In 2007, she took on the role of Newly Qualified Teacher Recruitment and Retention Officer. Currently she works with Julie Shaw in the Bi-Borough Education Service with joint responsibility for NQT (Newly Qualified Teacher) induction and Continuing Professional Development programmes.

Elizabeth N. King is working as a research psychologist for Children's Services in a large local authority in Scotland, UK. Elizabeth was previously Principal Psychologist for twenty years within the same authority. Research interests include bereavement, and Elizabeth and her team collaborated for over a decade with MacMillan Cancer Support to develop and research the impact of a group work programme for young people experiencing bereavement and loss.

Julie Shaw qualified as an Early Years teacher at the Institute of Early Childhood Studies, College of Advanced Education (now Macquarie University), Australia. Since 2011, Julie has been Newly Qualified Teacher (NQT) Coordinator working closely with Linda Crichton. Together Julie and Linda manage and quality assure the NQT induction (post qualification professional accreditation) process for around 300 beginning teachers each academic year.

Matthew Somerville is Lecturer in Psychology at the UCL Institute of Education, University College London, UK, and Programme Leader of the MSc Psychology of Education degree programme. He is also a Registered Practitioner Psychologist in the UK and a Registered Educational Psychologist in New Zealand/Aotearoa. His research interests are concerned with educational contexts that support children's social and emotional development with a primary focus on emotion regulation and how it relates to mental health and well-being.

Stuart Woodcock is Associate Professor at Griffith University, Australia, in inclusive education and educational psychology in the School of Education and Professional Studies. Stuart initially trained as a teacher in England. Since then he has taught in England, Canada and Australia in primary and secondary schools. Stuart's established research areas focus on inclusive education, classroom and behaviour management, and, teacher self-efficacy not only within Australia but also the UK, North America and China.

Acknowledgements

We would like to thank the following people for their assistance and contributions in many forms to this volume – Estelle Bryant, Sara Darchicourt, Julie Ely, Sam Habal, Ian Heggs, Helen Kerslake, Lucy Nutt, Jane Roller and Richard Stanley. We wish to also thank the 2017–18 cohort of Newly Qualified Teachers based across Kensington and Chelsea, Hammersmith and Fulham and Westminster Local Authorities in London and the NQTs working in a large secondary school in Kent. Their invaluable assistance in various focus groups in the early stages of developing this book was most helpful.

Last, but not least:

Jeremy Monsen wishes to thank – Stewart Clark, Barbara Monsen, Michelle Monsen, Nicholas Monsen and Angela Smidt for all their support and teaching over many years.

Lisa Marks Woolfson wishes to thank her wonderful family. That's Drs Tessa and Fergal Davis, Esther, Seth and Orla; Eve and Dr David Brill, Sylvie, Ted and Raya; and of course Dr Richard Woolfson, for all their love, support, encouragement, for making her laugh lots, and for teaching her new things every day.

James Boyle would like to specially thank Dr Liz Boyle, and their sons, daughters-in-law and seven grandchildren for their love and support during writing and editorial work on this book.

Abbreviations

AAC	Augmentative and Alternative Communication
AfA	Achievement for All
AGT	Able, Gifted and Talented
AIDS	Acquired immunodeficiency syndrome
AR	Augmented Reality
ASC	Autism Spectrum Condition
ASD	Autism Spectrum Disorder
BSL	British Sign Language
ChYPMHS	Children's and Young People Mental Health Services
CPD	Continuing Professional Development
CQC	Care Quality Commission
CRPD	Convention on the Rights of Persons with Disabilities
DfE	Department of Education
DMD	Duchenne Muscular Dystrophy
DME	Dual and/or Multiple Exceptionalities
DoH	Department of Health
EADSNE	European Agency for the Development of Special Education
EP	Educational Psychologist
EY	Early Years
G&T	Gifted and Talented
GT	Gifted and Talented
HIV	human immunodeficiency virus
HoC	House of Commons
HPL	High Potential Learning
ICT	Information and communication technology
ITE	Initial Teacher Education
LAC	Looked After Child (by the State)
LD	Learning Difficulties
NAO	National Audit Office
NQT	Newly Qualified Teacher
OECD	Organization for Economic Co-operation and Development
Ofsted	Office for Standards in Education
OHCHR	Office of the High Commissioner for Human Rights

OT	Occupational Therapist
PBIS	Positive Behaviour Interventions and Support
PECs	Picture Exchange Communications System
PhET	Physics Education Technology
PPEO	Policy, Practice (provision), Experiences, and Outcomes
Primary School	Equivalent to Elementary School in the United States, covering ages of about 5–10
PRU	Pupil Referral Unit
SALT	Speech and Language Therapist
SAMR	Substitution, Augmentation, Modification and Redefinition
SDG	Sustainable Development Goals
Secondary School	Equivalent to Junior High and High School in USA, covering ages roughly 11–18 years
SETT	Student Environment Tasks Tools
SEMH	social, emotional and mental health
SEN	Special Educational Needs
SENCo	Special Educational Needs Coordinator
SEND	Special Educational Needs and Disabilities
SLCD	Speech, Language and/or Communication Difficulties
SNA	Special Need Assistant
SpLD	Specific Learning Difficulty
SRP	Specialist Resource Provision
TA	Teaching Assistant
TEACCH	Teaching, Expanding, Appreciating, Collaborating and Cooperating, and Holistic
UD	Universal Design
UDL	Universal Design Learning
UN	United Nations
UNCRC	UN Convention on the Rights of the Child
UNESCO	United Nations Educational, Scientific and Cultural Organization
UNICEF	United Nations International Children's Emergency Fund
VLL	Virtual Learning Lab
VOCA	Voice Output Communication Aid
VR	Virtual reality
WHO	World Health Organization

1

Setting the Context

Jeremy Monsen, Lisa Marks Woolfson and James Boyle

Sylvia Ashton-Warner, an inspirational New Zealand teacher, often stressed in her talks and conversations with teachers that they must be true to themselves. Strong enough to be true to themselves. Brave enough to be strong enough to be true to themselves. Wise enough to be brave enough to be strong enough to shape themselves from what they actually are.

Setting the scene

There is a view that teachers are born rather than made, and that teaching is more of a 'craft' than an evidenced-based discipline. Some teachers come into the profession because they feel it is a core part of who they are as a person, a really important vocation, in the religious sense of the term. Others passionately recall that 'one great teacher' they had who inspired them for all kinds of different reasons. Often such people attempt to model their own image of themselves as a teacher off that person. The reality is often very different and far more complicated (Korthagen, 2004, 2010).

> **Reflexive question**
> You might want to pause at this early stage and think about your own motivation for becoming a teacher. What were your real reasons (you don't have to tell anyone!) – one of your parents was a teacher; you had a sibling with special educational needs and wanted to make a difference; you could not think of anything else to do after university; the holidays seemed excellent; you wanted to be like your favourite teacher and inspire others; or something else?

Our reasons and motivations for wanting to teach are often very personal and can be many and varied and are not necessarily all based on elevated ideals or lofty principles. It is important to be honest with yourself.

Some of the themes that underpin this volume may challenge some of the preconceptions around the development of a competent teacher and what constitutes effective practice. Teaching increasingly involves the active use of **research** mediated through a teacher's own critical thinking to improve pupil attainment, and wider social-emotional development, including mental health and well-being. This is the 'new' scientist-practitioner role advocated by a range of authors (Hattie, 2009, 2012; Kelly and Perkin, 2012; Kennedy and Monsen, 2016; Monsen and Woolfson, 2012; Robinson, 1993; Sato and Loewen, 2018).

Crucially, we argue that teachers can be developed and nurtured and carry on doing so across their careers no matter what their initial motivations or reasons were for entering the profession. Teachers can do this by gaining insights into their underlying attitudes and beliefs, by trying out new ways of thinking and behaving, and so evolve new skills and ways of doing things in the classroom and wider school community. We view **practice supervision** (and the coaching model detailed in this chapter) as being a core component in the process of becoming a truly 'reflective practitioner' and an effective teacher (Schön, 1983, 1987).

During initial teacher training programmes, whether primarily university or field based, the core role of practice supervision involving opportunities for receiving feedback, then reflecting upon it and planning new solutions, is not questioned. Yet as teachers become more experienced often this important professional development activity gets marginalized and somehow diminished. Not because teachers see supervision as being inherently unimportant, but other day-to-day prosaic tasks seem to take precedence.

To be effective, teachers must be honest with themselves about what attitudes and beliefs underpin their thinking and subsequent actions within the classroom when working with pupils and relating to others. This is important if they want to identify their potential biases, and effectively design new ways of thinking and acting to improve their applied practice (Darling-Hammond, 2006).

The importance of feedback

According to Darling-Hammond (2006), self-reflection, and by association, professional learning is dependent upon the quality of feedback you as a teacher receive. Feedback guides your understanding of your practice and what underpins it, while at the same time connecting your prior knowledge, learning, and experience with new insights and understandings.

Reflection can be seen as being an active process involving the interrogation of your thinking and actions with the motivation to take responsibility to understand and improve your applied practice. But you cannot do this task on your own, you need another person to act as your 'critical friend' to help inform and guide this process (Shoffner et al., 2010).

Reflexive questions

1. Have you ever felt defensive at someone's feedback about your teaching practice?
2. What thoughts and feelings were going through your head?

Reflective questions

1. What did the person do and say that made you choose to feel defensive?
2. What has been your experience to date of supervision?
3. What things make it an effective and/or ineffective approach for you?

Guided reflection and the coaching relationship

The coaching relationship is one way to enable guided self-reflection within supervision to occur effectively and safely (Cameron and Monsen, 1998; Hobson, 2016; Kearney, 1994; Lynch, 2014; Monsen and Cameron, 2002; Smith and Lynch, 2014; Stahl, Sharplin and Kehrwald, 2016; Vikaraman, Mansor and Hamzah, 2017).

It is important to stress that the dynamic we are describing is separate to wider institutional line management supervision which is equally important but serves different organizational purposes and functions. Practice supervision can involve two (or more) people of the same or different level of experience or competence. The important elements are knowing who is taking on the 'supervisor' and 'supervisee' roles in any interchange (this can alternate as required) and for both parties to utilize a shared process framework. In this chapter we describe and offer the coaching model as one way to structure and guide such conversations (Cameron and Monsen, 1998; Monsen and Cameron, 2002).

This said, Cevik, Haslaman and Celik (2015) found that peer feedback alone was not sufficient to scaffold teacher's critical reflections. Their research highlights the importance, certainly within the first few years of teaching practice, of linking oneself to a more experienced practitioner. At the same time it does not preclude obtaining and integrating feedback from students, peers, parents/carers and other colleagues, but the anchoring relationship needs to be between the supervisee and supervisor. Or indeed it might be better considered as a relationship between a coach and coachee with less hierarchical and managerial connotations implied (Cameron and Monsen, 1998).

Research shows that providing high-quality feedback to a coachee when in the coach role can be fraught with many challenges (Bullough et al., 2002). Glenn (2006) identified the apprehensions among supervisors about delivering what could be perceived as critical or negative feedback. For your purposes this could be reframed more constructively as the supervisor illuminating and offering a perspective based as closely as possible on observable information and allowing any subsequent attributions to be jointly explored. Such feedback could, for example, follow a classroom observation of a particular lesson, delivering training to the whole staff or sitting in on a parent–carer–teacher feedback session, and provides a view on the match or mismatch between what the teacher said they did (or would do) and what actually occurred (or could happen) and the intended and unintended consequences on the self, others and the environment (Argyris and Schön, 1974, 1996; also see Chapter 5 in this volume which develops these core concepts much further as a guide to developing more effective interpersonal communication when dealing with challenging encounters). Such feedback framed in this way is the stimulus for practitioner reflective thinking.

Dewey (1933) suggested that reflective thinking involves five aspects:

(i) A felt difficulty (*or that uneasy feeling that a lesson did not go as well as you had thought, despite over planning and using lots of materials*); (ii) its location and definition (*or the importance of being clear what actually occurred before, during and after rather than over generalising and saying 'I'm a very good teacher'. Often issues are setting specific and it is important to be clear*); (iii) suggestion of possible solution (*or exploring how other ways of acting could have led to different outcomes. This is often where a coach can be most helpful in prompting a list of options*); (iv) development by reasoning of the bearings of the suggestion (*or with your coach critically explore best fit options from your previous list and exploring any unintended consequences*); (v) further observation and experiment leading to its acceptance or rejection; that is, the conclusion of belief or disbelief (*or often the most effective interventions are simple, focused, and time limited and open to review and change over time*).

(Dewey, 1933, p. 72)

At its core reflective thinking is the temporary suspension of judgement to allow for active inquiry to determine what the nature of the problem actually is before rushing in with a solution which may or may not address the underlying dynamics (Robinson, 2018).

Yet it appears to be common practice, certainly within educational institutions, for people to spend little if any time really gaining feedback or reflecting upon their actions (or those of others) to any real extent and clarifying situations before adopting interventions or making changes. This is often raised as one reason some educational reforms are not effective (see Fullan, 2010 and the evaluation of National Literacy and Numeracy Hour programmes rolled out across England in the late 1990s; Robinson, 2018).

Piaget's concept of dis-equilibrium is very useful here to illustrate such a common human dilemma (Inhelder and Piaget, 1958). It stresses that part of the learning process involves uncomfortable feelings and learning to live, for a time at least, with uncertainty whilst clarifying complex situations and dynamics before moving to a new state of equilibrium and balance, and being ready for the next episode of uncertainty. It is giving yourself permission that you do not have to solve everything immediately and that time spent feeling 'uncomfortable' is part of the creative problem-solving process, so you need to learn to acknowledge and go with these moments (Pound, 2006; Robinson, 2018).

This line of reasoning leads Dewey to suggest that professional learning is the reconstruction and the reorganization of our lived experiences. In fact, Dewey believed that such a process becomes a 'habit of action', as a result of adopting the scientific method within applied practice or what is now referred to as the scientist-practitioner stance (Dewey, 1929; Kelly and Perkins, 2012; Kennedy and Monsen, 2016).

Schön (1987), building upon Dewey's ideas, acknowledges the central importance of reflection in practice development. He describes two main modes; first is – *reflection-on-action* which involves reflecting on how practice can be developed (changed) after the event 'we reflect on action, thinking back on what we have done in order to discover how our knowing-in-action may have contributed to an unexpected outcome' (Schön, 1987, p. 26).

But Schön (1983) also highlights the importance of a second mode – *reflection-in-action*. This he describes as reflecting on the incident whilst it can still benefit that situation rather than reflecting on how you would do things differently in the future. This is a useful tool to use in disciplines like teaching where the practitioner has to react to an event at the time it occurs, rather than having the luxury of being able to think about what happened and make changes at a later stage. Real-world dilemmas, unlike laboratory puzzles, are never so clear cut, organized or controllable.

Schön (1983, p. 68) suggests that 'when someone reflects-in-action … (they) become a researcher in the practice context. … (are) not dependent on the categories or established theory and technique but constructs a new theory of the unique case'.

In this sense then you as a teacher are an applied scientist, you will need to analyse complex situations; utilize experience and research to inform predications about the consequences of your actions and those of others; you will need to plan for and set up new ways of responding and see what affects you have on yourself, the pupils, other colleagues and parents/cares; as a teacher you will refine what works and discard what does not and learn as you go along so that the next time you encounter a similar issue you have a script or framework to deal with it, or at least guide you in the initial stages of managing it.

Some might see this as a teacher's 'craft knowledge' which implies a degree of intuition and automaticity. We would stress that the additional cognitive component of guided critical reflection and active problem-solving distinguishes the two related processes.

Table 1.1 Framework to guide the coaching process and relationship (GROWER model)

Goal phase – Understand the coachee's work context, current problem situation, summarize and agree working goal(s)	
Step 1	Review Coaching Contract (roles, purpose, location, time [normally an hour per session], confidentiality) and give Coachee their version of the Coaching Record Form.
Step 2	Obtain a 'rich picture' of the work context and the current problem through open questioning ('Tell me more about that?', 'What did you mean by that?').
Step 3	Paraphrase sections of the Coachee's statement of the current problem ('So from what I have heard you are concerned about you classroom behaviour management and what parents are thinking of you, is that correct?').
Step 4	Reflect back not only their thoughts but emotions/feelings (if appropriate) ('Listening to you I felt that you were feeling slightly overwhelmed?').
Step 5	Clarify the current problem with closed questions ('So am I correct that we are going to explore how to improve both your understanding and approach to classroom behaviour management?').
Step 6	Provide a brief summary and agree the current problem to be worked on ('So today we are going to explore some of the assumptions and perceptions you have been making about how you and parents are seeing your classroom management?' 'You want to feel at the end of the process more in control and that you feel parents are more appreciative and less critical?').
Step 7	Agree a set of clear objectives for the session and longer term aims (if appropriate).
Reality phase – Examine systemic aspects and develop a shared understanding	
Step 8	Invite comments on any systemic factors which might support or reduce the current problem (relationships with senior management, parents/carers, other colleagues, perceived expectations).

Step 9	Identify any systemic changes that might be required (clarify around school policy on classroom behaviour management).
Step 10	Explicitly check out their coherence, relevance and validity.
Step 11	Carefully check out any untested assumptions or attributions which seem to be being made (self, others, environment) ('So how do you know that?').
Step 12	Discuss and log any systemic issues which appear substantive, however keep the focus on areas which the Coachee has direct power to act and can make changes.

Options phase – Consider underlying coachee relevant dimensions critically explore selected dimensions

Step 13	Explore the current problem (as agreed) suggest connections/themes, highlight mismatches, unpack apparently hidden agendas, point out gaps in expertise/knowledge, and identify key conflict areas.
Step 14	Provide a brief summary and then invite possible dimensions from the Coachee to work on (list these) (lack of confidence, lack of techniques/strategies, worried about what parents think, worried about what senior management think, fear of failure).
Step 15	Reflect on the Dimensions list generated.
Step 16	Ask the Coachee to select one/two Core Dimensions to work on during the session(s).

Wrap-up phase – Agree an action plan

Step 17	Create a menu of possible concrete choices in the form of an Action Plan.
Step 18	Offer additional possibilities carefully.
Step 19	Carry out a cost-benefit analysis of the Action Plan.
Step 20	Consider possible unintended consequences as well and intended, constraints and pitfalls (role-play/rehearse/develop scripts if helpful).
Step 21	Critically discuss expected outcomes and processes to measure impact of Action Plan.

Evaluation phase – Evaluating outcomes/processes

Step 22	Review Action Plan and identify what went well/not so well and why?
Step 23	Consider what was learned.
Step 24	Consider what to do differently next time.
Step 25	Reflect on any development needs for the Coachee which emerged from the outcomes of their Action Plan.

Reflection phase – The coaching process and relationship

Step 26	Identify assets of the coaching session(s).
Step 27	Identify areas for improvement to coaching session(s).
Step 28	Review coaching arrangements (the Coaching Contract).
Step 29	Reflect on any development needs for the coach emerging from the coaching session(s).

Adapted from the model described by Cameron and Monsen (1998), Monsen and Cameron (2002) and Whitmore (2009).

Teacher coaching

Coaching provides a process framework which enables the class or subject teacher to step back from complex problem situations, examine these more objectively and generate new ways of thinking and acting. For you as a teacher the coaching framework provides a straightforward and safe way of structuring the complex reflective thinking task.

Two people agree to meet with one member adopting a 'coachee', and the other colleague a 'coach' role. They agree to explore using a shared framework (see Table 1.1 which offers one approach). They agree to explore in depth the factors underlying a particular problem or dilemma of practice which the coachee has encountered in their classroom or wider school context, and is bringing to that particular coaching session.

Such explorations will include not only a closer examination of the problem context (the setting, the people, the dynamics, the constraints, the possible opportunities), but the coachee's personal attitudes, beliefs and perspectives and the extent to which these can reduce, maintain or indeed exacerbate particular problem situations (Cameron and Monsen, 1998).

The coaching process described by Cameron and Monsen (1998) and Monsen and Cameron (2002) and presented in Table 1.1 was initially based on the work of Kearney (1995, influenced by sports coaching, Lyle, 2002; Lyle and Cushion, 2017) but was further developed for use with educational and child psychologists and teachers. It is more suited to the needs of teachers, than the sports coaching model, especially since it focuses less on skills development and more on emphasizing active reflection of one's thinking, actions and their consequences. It enables teachers to explore and understand organizational, interpersonal and individual dynamics which they may experience within the classroom and beyond. The use of the acronym 'GROWER' as a short hand way of summarizing the model was influenced by the work of Whitmore (2009).

This framework can allow the coachee to gain additional insight into the nature of such dynamics, permit a consideration of controlling factors and promote the generation of alternative strategies which can then be turned into an action plan. Such a plan can enable the teacher to manage a persistent or complex problem situation more successfully.

For both coach and coachee, learning can take place both at a micro-level (reflective) (better strategies for managing a particularly difficult issue within the classroom or wider school environment) and at a macro-level (reflexive) (reflecting on insights into beliefs, attitudes and constructs which may have emerged from the coaching process and could be unintentionally supporting less effective actions).

The following excerpt of a teacher's abridged notes following a coaching session gives a flavour of the types of issues, understandings and insights that the coaching process can help illuminate for the coachee. Such insights can lead to new ways of thinking, acting and feeling.

Case study: Excerpt from an abridged coaching record

Country: UK

Age group: Secondary/High school level

Setting: Mainstream state/public maintained school

Participant involved: Ben Khan (coachee) is in his third year of teaching and has had a coaching session with the school's link Educational Psychologist

Background and presenting themes

I'm currently working as a Senior Teacher (Acting) in a Pupil Referral Unit (PRU) attached to a large mainstream secondary/high school. A PRU is a special class for pupils who are finding managing their behaviour within mainstream classrooms a challenge. It provides smaller class sizes, and more individualized work and support.

I was transferred to the Unit, which consists of three classes from my main position as a Physical Education teacher late last year because there were ongoing staffing shortages within the Unit. The Head-teacher and the Head of the PRU thought I would be excellent for the position and indicated that if it worked out the promoted post would be mine. In terms of career progression, increased responsibilities and salary it would represent a significant advancement for me.

During the coaching session the coach offered a range of reflections and themes (Problem Dimensions) after listening to my 'problem story'. The following insights particularly resonated with me – (a) 'that I did not do my homework around what the job actually involved. I did not observe or shadow in the Unit but impulsively agreed because I felt flattered by the Head-teacher and Head of Unit', (b) 'I seem to have a need for people and pupils to like me and this can influence how I deal with relationships and situations' and (c) 'I seem to have forgotten all of the teaching strategies I used whilst teaching PE and am finding it very stressful managing the pupils challenging behaviour'.

The main reason I decided to try coaching was my increasing feelings of frustration, disappointment and sense that unless I changed retaining this position was not likely to happen.

These themes were explored further with the priority goal being: 'How do I manage challenging adolescent behaviour more effectively?'

Issues, thoughts and reflections

1. The pupils in my class are all aged between fourteen and fifteen years and are presenting with significant behavioural, social-emotional and well-being needs. Mainly conduct and attachment issues. Given their backgrounds and developmental stages, their challenging behaviours should not have been a surprise to me. On hindsight my preparation could have been much more thorough. I could have talked to Unit staff about how they managed such pupils, observed in other PRU classes, read pupil files, got to know them as individuals, and identified what their primary needs and strengths were.
2. It was hard for me to acknowledge but as I tried to make the pupils like me the opposite occurred. They did not listen to me, ignored me, were rude and answered back. I have now started to shout at the pupils. I think that some colleagues and parents/carers have heard me, but have said nothing directly to me. A friend from the PE Department said that a parent/carer asked them if I was 'alright' but did not elaborate.
3. I need to reconnect to sound first principles around classroom behaviour management and organization, request support and guidance from my line manager, and importantly tell them how I am feeling and what I need. It seems that my pride has stopped me from doing this, as has my tendency to make assumptions about how they and others see me and act as if those views were true. I need to move from seeing myself as a failure to someone who genuinely wants to learn to be a better teacher.
4. I feel embarrassed, disappointed and a bit of a failure. In terms of empowering me to make changes such thinking is not particularly helpful. Through weekly coaching sessions and the input of my line manager I will need to challenge some of my unhelpful thinking processes and reframe my experiences so that I can think about and do things differently.

This then led to an exploration of possible strategies I could implement.

Possible ideas and strategies explored during the session:

1. I realize that I need to re-establish my relationship with the pupils and set in place clearer boundaries and classroom structures. My main aim is not to be liked but for the pupils to feel safe and grounded, and to respect me and see that I am

motivated to helping them learn and develop as people. Gaining some emotional distance between the pupils and myself so that I can restore some objectivity will be important to me. The weekly coaching sessions should aid this process.

2. I will make an attempt to try and focus on the times pupils are behaving 'adequately' ('catch them being good' idea) and quietly let them know (specific praise statements, gestures, facial expressions, rewards and incentive systems). I plan to continue to use the tally system on my watchstrap to record my attention to both positive and negative behaviours. At the moment I am focusing almost exclusively on negative pupil behaviour. This approach was recommended by my coach as part of preparation for the session and as a baseline. What really struck me was how inconsistent I have been with the class, one minute being 'nice' (but not authentic) and the next minute trying to be firm and yet resorting to shouting. I need to be a lot more honest and consistent with the class. Equally I need to be a lot more honest with my line manager as I am assuming they know how I feel and what I need.

3. I will read all pupil files and subsequently conduct individual interviews so that I can get a clearer picture of how they are making sense of things. This may well help me to gain some insight into how to motivate and connect with them as individuals. I explored the idea of building upon my strengths as a Kendo instructor. Teaching the class the discipline of Kendo could be used effectively with these pupils as it could develop self-discipline, a sense of achievement and challenge, working together as a team, burning up energy and focusing on a non-academic activity as part of a daily programme.

4. I need to spend more time in preparing for lessons so I have engaging and motivating content and structure. I have mainly been reactive and have not thought fully about the power of the curriculum to provide external structure and order (having a range of approaches, whole class, small groups and some one-to-one sessions).

A successful coaching contract

As well as having a framework (Table 1.1) to guide the coaching relationship that is both explicit and transparent, a number of other important aspects to the coaching relationship need to be considered. It is important to recognize issues which are outside the competence (or professional comfort zone) of the coach; avoid the development of co-dependency; maintain confidentiality; discuss the appropriate level of self-disclosure; manage and modulate the expression of strong emotions; maintain the support-versus-challenge balance in coaching sessions; agree ownership of any notes taken during the coaching session; decide on the type of coaching arrangement (hierarchical versus peer and/or group) and the time commitment required.

As the coaching relationship develops, it will be necessary to revisit some of the issues listed in the previous paragraph. Therefore, a joint evaluation should be built into the coaching process. Evaluation issues could include:

- Feedback from coachee to coach on the benefits/drawbacks of the coach's style.
- A revision of the contract terms (using the issues list from the previous paragraph).
- A short feedback session on how coaching advice was used/adapted in practice.
- The implications of the above for the coach and coachee's practice development.

The strategy of coaching, and the critical guided reflection which underpins it, typically tends to have a personal (and often private) effect. Some thought may therefore need to be given to identifying demonstrable outcomes. First of all, the coachee may be encouraged to articulate subtle shifts that have taken place in their belief system. For example, Ben in the case study shared earlier might say:

> *I used to think that being liked by my students was key to my role and when I began to have issues with classroom management it really hurt me. It was as if they were rejecting me. I now have learnt that my authority as a teacher and subsequent student respect is actually in the way that I influence learners and not just a focus on being liked, this has made a big difference.*

Such qualitative data are important since it can provide evidence of the impact of a coaching session on an individual.

At a more quantitative level, observable change can be identified. For example, Ben might be able to highlight the changes in practice which have accompanied their cognitive shift, by noting that more time is now spent on lesson planning, preparation and classroom structure/boundaries and rules, and encouraging students to take more personal responsibility for the consequences of their choices rather than behaviours designed to curry favour with the students. Clearly, these are behaviours that can be measured.

Coaching is not counselling

Superficially coaching and counselling seem to share common features and outcomes. Counselling has been described as assisting a person to take on more responsibility for the consequences of their choices and their actions (Nelson-Jones, 2014). This is particularly so when they are involved in difficult situations which they are not acknowledging or managing that well (Egan, 2014). Importantly the person must have the desire to want to try to become more effective at solving their personal, social and emotional dilemmas (Dryden, 2019).

The major distinction between coaching and counselling is the means of achieving personal learning objectives. In particular, the coaching framework is more detailed, and the role of the coach is more directive. The focus of coaching is upon work-related issues and the action plan is likely to be more structured and detailed than in the case of a counselling session. Most of all, the relationship between coach and coachee is likely to be less hierarchical than in counselling interactions. The coachee retains a high level of control over the content of the coaching session, the exploration of particular problem dimensions and any action chosen. They can be seen to be driving the process.

Reflective questions

1. What do you need to do to set up and develop a coaching partnership in your current school?
2. Who do you need to involve, what practice do you both need and how will you know it is achieving its goal?

Window on research

Developing student teachers' teaching self-efficacy through Shared Mentoring in Learning Environments (SMILE)

Another support programme was developed by Chizhik and colleagues (2018) and it is a student teacher mentoring model called Shared Mentoring in Learning Environments (SMILE). It was developed to enable university-based teacher trainers and classroom practitioners to collaborate and build shared understandings when mentoring student teachers. SMILE adopts the Japanese approach of using 'lesson study' to facilitate teacher development. Lesson study involves teachers collaborating together to plan lessons by watching a member of the group devise a lesson, providing feedback and implementing changes based on that feedback (Perry and Lewis, 2009). Lesson study involves teachers working together to improve student learning, which is known as a Professional Learning Community (PLC).

Chizhik and colleagues (2018) research team investigated the SMILE model on a sample of student teachers to compare teaching efficacy with a group of student teachers mentored using a more traditional approach. The SMILE teachers met with their university-based trainers (supervisor) and classroom teacher to discuss lesson plans. Each PLC group comprised two student teachers, their university trainer (supervisor) and their classroom teachers. During the meetings the student teachers discussed their lesson plans with the group who provided feedback on how to improve each lesson. Student teachers used the feedback from the meetings to revise their lesson plans, which were video recorded. They then shared these video clips with their PLCs to emphasize the issues that were discussed in the first PLC meeting. During the second meeting, members of the group offered strengths and suggestions, to further improve the student teacher's learning. Using feedback from the video recordings, the student teachers made adjustments to their lessons which were then observed by their university supervisors, who provided further feedback. This process was called smile rotation, with the students having four smile rotations throughout the academic year, with each rotation focusing on a different issue (classroom management; delivering complex lesson content).

The study found that student teachers in the SMILE group reported an improvement in their teaching efficacy compared to those in the traditional mentoring group. In addition, they found that students in the SMILE group found critical feedback helpful and felt that it had improved their teaching efficacy. Furthermore, student teachers in the SMILE condition attributed their improvement in teaching skills to the mentoring from their university supervisors and classroom teachers. However, student teachers in the traditional group attributed their improvement mainly to the classroom teacher.

Overall, the findings suggest that the SMILE model can be useful in improving student teacher's learning by incorporating the feedback roles of both the university-based supervisor and classroom teacher. It might have value being introduced across a whole school staff with large numbers of beginning teachers and could generate economies of scale and provide a development to one-on-one coaching.

This book

The previous sections focused on the importance of feedback and optimal relationships for receiving it. Feedback of course is a key concept in psychology. Think, for example, of the lectures and courses you have had on summative and formative assessment during your teacher training or Continuing Professional Development (CPD). The discipline of psychology has underpinned educational practice since its inception and teacher-training courses typically involve psychology modules. This book aims to help you as a teacher by showing you how and where psychology can be applied beyond the training period, and how this will benefit your continuing practice. The book explains why it is every teacher's responsibility to know about the powerful effects that psychology can deliver.

It will make explicit the links between psychological theory, research, practical strategies and your own developing identity as a teacher. Its emphasis is on personal, social and emotional perspectives. As well as educational and developmental psychology, we will utilize findings from work psychology, health psychology and the related counselling literature. Each chapter will make use of one or two case studies to highlight dilemmas and issues that teachers might encounter in their practice. There will be 'Window on research' where we explain in more detail a research study or a concept that further develops a theme explored in the chapter.

Rather than providing you with a 'cookbook' of teaching tips, our focus here is on your needs in practice. We aim to enable you to:

- understand and develop confidence in your role as a teacher, so that you can work effectively with pupils, parents/carers and other colleagues.
- develop an understanding of your role, and practical strategies to overcome barriers to effective working and applied practice.

The book will explore the context of often polarized debates around whether teaching is an evidence-based profession or a craft, as well as the historical and contemporary settings within which teaching occurs. Within this context comes the need to recognize that effective classroom practice involves an acknowledgement by you and every teacher of your own needs in order to ensure you maintain your own mental health and well-being. Questions are provided in each chapter to allow personal reflection on the issues and dilemmas highlighted. There will be emphasis throughout on practical strategies.

In **Chapter 2** we identify seven key roles and responsibilities for teachers: teaching, pastoral, development and training, collegial working, communication, citizenship and ethos, and administration. These wide-ranging and challenging roles extend beyond the classroom and encompass not only the traditional, 'occupational' view of the profession characterized by autonomy and trust, but also an 'organizational' view which takes into account the increasing demands of hierarchical management structures with their emphasis upon accountability, performance review and standardization of classroom teaching practice and learning.

These roles and responsibilities provide a context for considering the formation and development of teacher professional identity and links with pupil achievement and engagement, and teacher stress and retention rates. The concept of teacher professional identity and complexities in its definition are considered in the light of contributions from the perspectives of role identity, social identity and 'figured worlds' theories. A review of the research literature supports the view that teacher professional identity is fluid, and socially constructed from narratives and discourse, and develops over the course of a career by processes of construction and reconstruction informed by feedback and negotiation. Evidence for a relationship between effective teaching, job satisfaction, well-being and commitment to the profession on the one hand, and teacher self-efficacy and positive and supportive relationships with colleagues and school leaders on the other, is discussed. Implications for teachers at all stages of their careers are considered.

In **Chapter 3** we deal with your health and well-being. The chapter will look at the developing role identity of teachers, managing possible role conflicts and maintaining professional roles, responsibilities and boundaries, burnout, stress, developing resilient attitudes and behaviour. The aim being to identify things teachers need to be consciously aware of so that they can make informed choices.

In **Chapter 4** we examine the social world of the classroom. The chapter begins by discussing the nature of the classroom environment and how the physical organization of the classroom, in terms of furniture, seating arrangements and available resources can influence the nature of pupils' interactions with both the teacher and their peers. Different forms of ability grouping are presented along with a discussion on how these groupings can have marked effects on pupil motivation and academic attainment. The chapter highlights the importance of teacher–pupil relationships and how interactions between and among teaching staff and pupils can influence a pupil's progress throughout their schooling. It looks at relationships and interactions among peers – an area that has received relatively little attention when compared to the large body of work investigating teacher–pupil interactions. Finally, a discussion of cooperative and collaborative group work is presented, including an overview of the SPRinG project (Baines, Blatchford and Kutnick, 2016) which has used classroom-based research to examine the effectiveness of peer and interactive group work within typical classroom settings.

In **Chapter 5** we argue that a teacher's ability to effectively communicate and jointly problem-solve with a wide range of people, sometimes under difficult circumstances is a core practice skill. Just having more experience alone is not sufficient to enable teachers to develop their skills. The chapter details the Accessible Dialogue framework. Once understood and practised it can be used to clarify what might underpin one's current communications style, provide a basis for testing out new ways of acting so different and more effective outcomes can occur. This chapter provides teachers with an outline of the theoretical basis underpinning the approach, its key components (framed in operational terms so they are easy to action and practice) and guidance on how to apply, gain feedback, reflect and develop skills over the course of their teaching careers.

In **Chapter 6** we acknowledge the central importance of teacher knowledge of the curriculum and subject areas but we go further and consider the skills and personal qualities and characteristics required to cope with the challenges and demands of teaching in the 2020s. Psychological theories and research identify and highlight the importance of the new 'three R's' of resilience, and the interrelated processes of reflection and reflexivity. Research evidence regarding resilience and coping with challenge and adverse, stressful situations, analytic skills of reflection-in-action, reflection-on-action and 'thinking about' experience through reflexivity are discussed in the light of attachment theory, transactional coping theory, biosocial theories of resilience, positive psychology, theories of critical thinking and experiential learning.

The implications for teachers' professional development and practice of awareness both of the impact of attachment history and of the importance of a questioning approach to experiential learning which takes into account the perspectives of others are discussed.

In **Chapter 7** we draw together key themes from the range of psychological frameworks and tools discussed across the previous chapters of this volume that impact upon the experience of being a teacher. The book concludes with ten practical next steps, suggestions to take forward regarding how to apply psychology to enhance the day-to-day experience of being a teacher.

Our intention throughout the book is to provide you as a teacher, and especially beginning teachers with psychological frameworks and practical strategies that will support you in your very important role. We believe passionately that you as a teacher have a significant influence on the lives of children and young people far beyond the time they are actually physically with you.

Annotated bibliography

Earl, L. M. and Timperley, H. (eds.) (2008). *Professional learning conversations: Challenges in using evidence for improvement (Professional learning and development in Schools and Higher Education).* **New York: Springer**.
This book will be of interest to those of you who want to explore in more depth how to undertake and embed educational change within your school or classroom. It explores how educators, policymakers and pupils try to rethink and change their practices by engaging in evidence-based conversations to challenge and guide their thinking and actions. It shares real conversations which enable you to see the processes talked about in action. The analysis of the conversations is revealing as they show the type of thinking that change requires and provides important insights into the process of critical reflection and the change process.

Hattie, J. (2009). *Visible learning: A synthesis of over 800 meta-analyses relating to achievement.* **Milton Park, UK: Routledge**.
For those of you who are interested in exploring further evidence-based research to inform your teaching practice we would recommend the work of Professor John Hattie. Hattie examined over 800 meta-analyses and identified ten of the most effective evidence-based teaching strategies that can be used within the classroom (these were – clear lesson goals/setting goals; structuring lessons; explicit teaching; worked examples; collaborative learning; multiple exposures; questioning; feedback; teaching metacognitive strategies and differentiated teaching). Hattie worked out the effect size for each intervention/strategy. Effect size in Hattie's study refers to how much an intervention contributes to improving student learning, which plays an important role in interpreting the effectiveness of teaching strategies. It is important to stress that the strategies should not be seen as

a simple 'check-list' but instead used along with other information to inform teacher thinking, reflection and problem-solving. Each classroom is unique and teachers need to actively reflect on what the issues are for them and what solutions they will explore and use (the scientist-practitioner model).

Neeman, M. and Dryden, W. (2013). *Life coaching: A cognitive behavioural approach.* **2nd edn. Abingdon, UK: Routledge.**

To support the development of your coaching skills we recommend this book by Michael Neeman and Windy Dryden. They share their many years of experience in working with people to solve work-related and personal problems. Their work is informed by cognitive behavioural approaches and they explore in more depth one of the core themes shared in this volume – that the way we think about situations influences the way we subsequently act and feel. So when working with a coachee to strive for better outcomes we need to help them think about themselves, others and the world in different and more constructive ways. With practice and hard work they will learn to think differently, leading to new ways of feeling and importantly acting on themselves, others and the world. Life Coaching shares many useful strategies that can be used to work with common coachee themes which emerge during sessions, such as – how to deal with self-defeating thinking, how to manage reoccurring troublesome emotions, how not to procrastinate so much, how to be more assertive, how to be better at time management, how to persist at problem-solving, how to handle criticism constructively, how to take calculated risks, how to make better decisions and how to develop greater resilience.

2

The Professional Self and Psychology

James Boyle, Jeremy Monsen and Lisa Marks Woolfson

As a classroom practitioner, how do you see yourself as 'a teacher'? Or, if you are a teacher in training or perhaps a teacher in the early stages of your career, what type of teacher do you aspire to be? To answer these questions, you need to consider 'teacher professional identity', or the professional 'self' – what it is to 'be' a teacher, how a teacher's understanding of their professional identity develops, what influences this development, and the impact of teacher professional identity upon job satisfaction, well-being and performance in the many roles and responsibilities that teachers are required to carry out (Beijaard et al., 2004).

It is possible to view 'identity' in a number of ways. There is a view that identity is not a trait that one 'has', but rather is socially constructed and shaped through negotiations and interactions with others over the course of life experience (Holland et al., 1998), highlighting the importance of language, narrative and discourse in the formation of identity. There is also agreement that it is helpful to distinguish between 'personal identity' (i.e. 'self' identity, the 'I', an internalized awareness and reflexive understanding of 'self' as a distinct individual) and 'group identity' (our understanding and awareness of 'self' in relation to others) with 'teacher professional identity' or the professional 'self' best understood as a form of group identity (Beijaard et al., 2004; Castells, 2010; Erikson, 1968; Hsieh, 2010). Of relevance here is the distinction drawn by Carl Rogers (1961) between our view of our 'real' or 'actual' self (who we feel that we 'really are', in terms of both our positive and negative qualities) and that of our 'ideal' self (the person that we strive to become in terms of our goals and ambitions). Our understandings of our 'real' and 'ideal' selves are shaped by the expectations of others and impact upon both personal and teacher professional identity; the greater the congruence between our real and ideal selves the higher our feelings of self-worth and the better able we are to deal with the challenges of both personal and professional lives (Ismail and Tekke, 2015).

The study of how teachers perceive and understand themselves has been of interest to educational researchers around the world addressing questions such as: What is the nature of teacher professional identity? How does it develop over the course of pre-service training and teaching career? Does teacher education play a part in its formation? Does professional identity have an impact upon the motivation and commitment of teachers? How does 'belonging' to a community of teachers impact upon professional identity? Does professional identity make a difference to how teachers 'teach' and to the effectiveness of their teaching?

Hsieh (2010, p. 1) defines teacher professional identity as 'the beliefs, values and commitments that allow a teacher to identify both as a teacher (distinct from other professional identities, e.g. doctor, accountant, architect) and as being a particular type of "teacher"'. Or as Brooke (1994) puts it, being a 'preschool teacher' rather than 'someone who teaches preschool'. However, teacher professional identity is also constructed in the light of roles and expectations laid down by society (Beijaard et al., 2004) and this has to be understood in terms of the practicalities of 'doing the job'.

In the first section of this chapter, therefore, the multifaceted roles and responsibilities of a teacher and what might constitute an 'effective teacher' are explored, before going on in the second section to consider how theories of 'self' and 'identity' from psychology and sociology can illuminate an understanding of teacher professional identity. We will also examine critically research evidence for links between the professional identity of the teacher and pupil achievement and engagement and effective teaching on the one hand, and between professional identify and 'burn-out', and teacher retention rates on the other. Finally, we will consider whether organizational and management processes, structures and supports in schools can make a difference to 'burn-out' and teacher retention rates and how beginning teachers especially can be supported to develop a positive sense of professional identity.

Roles and responsibilities of teachers

Everyone who has attended a school knows what a teacher 'does'. Personal history and life experience as a pupil gives the individual an understanding of the roles and responsibilities of a teacher, and indeed, teachers who made a positive difference to their life may have directly contributed to the career decision to train and practise as a teacher. Thus, everyone who has attended a school knows at some level what a teacher 'does' in a way that may be less true of most other professions. Lortie (2002) coined the term 'the apprenticeship of observation' to refer to the experience of spending years in classrooms as pupils with teachers. Individuals form judgements as a result of this period of extended apprenticeship about the practice of the teachers who made a difference, and perhaps also about the practice of those who were less effective (Malderez et al., 2007). These judgements may have informed a decision to become a teacher and also provided insights about 'how' to teach when the time came. Few other professions provide such a lengthy lived-in period of apprenticeship. Indeed, 'the apprenticeship of observation' continues for beginning teachers while they are in training and into their early years in the profession as they learn from watching the practice of experienced colleagues.

Yet this period of 'apprenticeship' may fail to capture the full range of the roles and responsibilities of a teacher. Direct experience as pupils of the learning, teaching and pastoral roles, for example, may lead to preconceptions resulting from a lack of awareness of the full range of the duties of teachers and the expectations placed upon them. Also, how might the job of a teacher in early education differ from that of a modern languages or physics teacher in a secondary school?

An online search of the Education Resource Information Centre (ERIC), the largest database of educational research publications, alone revealed over 26,000 publications on 'the role of the teacher' in the last ten years, so there is a considerable amount of information available. A number of websites from around the world list the roles of teachers (e.g. Eton Institute, n.d.; Guyana Ministry of Education, n.d.; SchoolNet SA, 2000; TEACH, n.d.) and indeed, for leaders in the teaching profession (Harrison and Killion, 2013). But such lists differ and the nature of the evidence upon which they are based is not always clear.

Accordingly, we used a case study approach to examine a sample of six job descriptions for vacancies for teacher posts in primary (Grades 1–6) and secondary schools (Grades 7–12) which were recently advertised in England. Such job

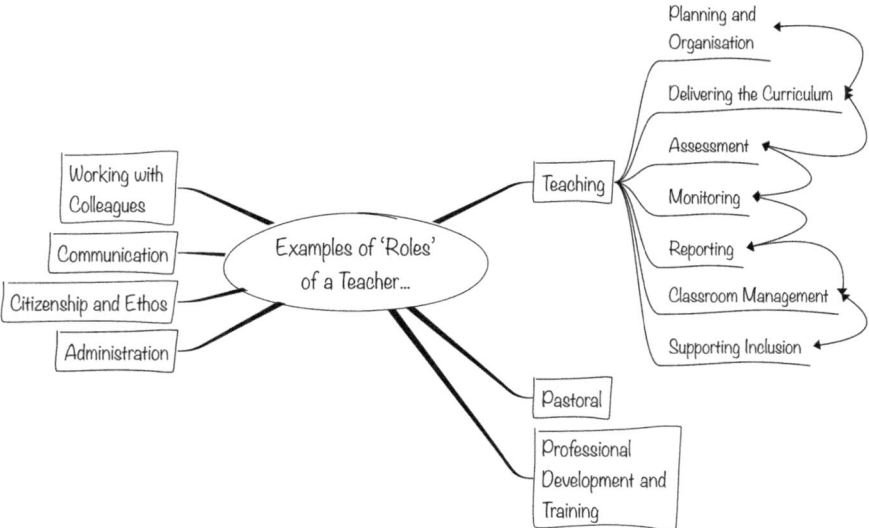

Figure 2.1 'Roles' of a teacher: findings from a thematic analysis of job descriptions.

descriptions detail roles and responsibilities which reflect current realities and expectations of the job and also its multifaceted roles.

The job descriptions sampled yielded 187 statements about the roles and responsibilities of teachers and these were analysed following the procedures for thematic analysis 'a method for identifying, analysing and reporting patterns (themes) within data' (Braun and Clarke, 2006, p. 79). A 'semantic' approach was used (i.e. analysing only the job description statements as provided rather than looking for any underlying 'latent' assumptions that employers may have had) and this identified seven recurring patterns, or 'themes', in the statements which correspond to the roles of a teacher, shown in Figure 2.1. These were: a 'teaching' role linked to seven areas of responsibility underpinning effective teaching and learning, a pastoral role, a professional development and training role, a role which entails working with colleagues, a communication role, a citizenship and ethos role, and finally, a role which entails administrative responsibilities.

Table 2.1 provides illustrative examples of the responsibilities of the 'teaching' role. The importance of planning lessons, of good organization and of delivering stimulating and interesting lessons linked to the needs of pupils, and of making learning appropriate, relevant and accessible, is held to underpin effective teaching and learning in the classroom (Bates, 2019; Castle and Buckler, 2018; Kington et al., 2014; Kyriacou, 2014). Beginning teachers in particular are expected to prepare lesson plans, which by demonstrating thought and reflection can help to build confidence in front of a class, as well as evidencing subject knowledge and understanding and skills of good organization.

Table 2.1 Responsibilities and illustrative examples of the role of 'Teaching'

Role	Responsibilities	Illustrative examples
'Teaching'	Planning and organization	• Planning, preparing and delivering lessons to all students in the class • To plan effectively to ensure pupils have the opportunity to meet their potential • Be responsible for the preparation and development of teaching materials and teaching programmes
	Delivering the curriculum	• Teaching according to the educational needs, abilities and achievement of the individual pupils and groups of pupils • Provide clear structures for lessons maintaining pace, motivation and challenge • To use teaching strategies that keep pupils engaged through effective questioning, lively presentation and good use of resources • Be aware of pupils' capabilities, their prior knowledge, and plan teaching and differentiate appropriately to build on these, thus demonstrating knowledge and understanding of how pupils learn

Assessment	• Assess and record pupils' progress systematically and keep records to check work is understood and completed, monitor strengths and weaknesses, inform planning and recognize the level at which the pupil is achieving • Assess how well learning objectives have been achieved and use outcomes to adapt teaching accordingly • Undertake assessment of pupils as requested by examination bodies, departmental and school procedures
Monitoring	• To monitor pupil's class and home activities, providing constructive oral and written feedback • Monitor (and set targets for) the social and academic progress of individuals in the class • Regularly review the effectiveness of teaching and assessment procedures and their impact on pupils' progress, attainment and well-being, refining approaches where necessary responding to advice and feedback from colleagues
Reporting	• Reporting on the development, progress, attainment and behaviour of pupils • Providing or contributing to oral and written reports and references relating to individual pupils or groups of pupils • To assess, record and monitor each pupil's progress in line with the curriculum and to report to parents
Classroom management	• Deploy a wide range of effective behaviour management strategies • Maintaining discipline in accordance with the school's procedures and encouraging good practice with regard to punctuality, behaviour, standards of work and homework • Implement rewards and sanctions within school policies and procedures
Supporting Inclusion	• Have a clear understanding of the needs of all pupils, including those with high academic, creative or physical and/or special educational needs and be able to use and evaluate distinctive teaching approaches to engage and support them • Be aware of and make provision for pupils who have special educational or additional support needs, or who have other particular individual needs

For Fullan and Langworthy (2014), one of the greatest challenges for the delivery of the curriculum, indeed for the teaching profession, is how to promote 'deeper' learning by pupils in the present digital era. They argue that this will require new pedagogies, tasks and challenges to best prepare pupils for their lives after school by helping them to develop skills such as thinking critically, thinking creatively, working collaboratively, communicating effectively and learning 'how' to learn.

Assessment, monitoring, reporting and feedback are also key elements of effective teaching, viewed as essential to ensure the appropriacy of the content of lessons and of how the content is being delivered (Bates, 2019; Hattie, 2012). Accurate assessment of progress towards a learning objective ('formative' assessment) and assessment at the end of a lesson to determine whether the objective has been achieved ('summative' assessment) are important means of monitoring pupils' progress which in turn inform lesson planning and target setting, as indicated by the bi-directional arrows in Figure 2.1. We can identify two further important types of assessment: 'inductive' assessment, often associated with curriculum-based assessment (Fuchs et al., 1994), where the assessment is used to determine the appropriacy of the learning objectives; and 'deductive' assessment, a summative assessment carried out at the end of a course as a review (Bates, 2019). Yet assessment need not have a narrow focus: it may also be understood as a more 'holistic' process (Cordingley et al., 2019), considering not only assessment of formal achievement outcomes but also assessment of the nature and quality of pupils' learning experiences and of the overall teaching and learning environment. In this vein, the importance of taking the perspectives of pupils into account in assessment and monitoring when determining the effectiveness of teaching and learning is key (Castle and Buckler, 2018).

Reporting is used to provide pupils with positive and fair feedback linked to expectations and individual needs and is also identified as a key component of effective teaching (Bates, 2019; Castle and Buckler, 2018; Gerson, 2015; Kington et al., 2014). Good feedback can encourage pupils to take ownership of their own learning and to develop self-efficacy (understanding and confidence in the ability to achieve goals) and self-regulation (the control of behaviour and emotions to achieve those goals) which motivate learners (Bandura, 1986).

Good classroom management is essential to the creation of a good environment for learning and is identified as a further prerequisite of effective teaching (Bates, 2019; Kington et al., 2014). The most common classroom problems are those of pupil chatter, calling out and being 'off-task' due to inattention, with more serious problems such as aggression towards teachers thankfully much less prevalent. There are many books dealing with the practicalities of managing a class (e.g. Bates, 2019; Canter and Canter, 1992; Rogers, 2015). In addition, in a recent chapter, Gulliford and Miller (2015) consider issues such as the role of motivation, discipline and control, of rewards and punishment, and of 'reactive' and 'preventative' approaches to classroom management and a school behaviour policy from the perspectives of behavioural psychological theory (e.g. the antecedents and consequences of behaviour), cognitive psychology (e.g. attribution theory), psychodynamic theory (e.g. attachment theory) and problem analysis, and reveal how an understanding of psychological theory can in turn contribute to understanding classroom behaviour and how to manage it.

The role of 'Supporting Inclusion' as defined here incorporates the appropriate, differentiated teaching strategies allied to the subject knowledge required to meet the individual needs of a broad range of learners, including those with special educational needs and needs for additional support. Again, such expertise is a hallmark of an effective teacher not only in a specialist setting, but also in mainstream classrooms (Brownell et al., 2009; Conderman and Johnston-Rodriguez, 2009; Lambert and Frederickson, 2015).

Responsibilities subsumed under the 'pastoral' role of a teacher are given in Table 2.2. These include fostering self-esteem and encouraging acceptance and respect for others (Scottish Government, 2019), dealing with problems of bullying and cyberbullying (Espelage et al., 2018; Smith, 2016; Ttofi and Farrington, 2010), tackling the problems of non-attendance and truancy (Gulliford and Miller, 2015a; Lauchlan, 2003) and supporting pupils in an age-appropriate way through life events such as bereavement and loss (Cohen et al., 2011; Holland, 2016), mental health issues (Castle and Buckler, 2018; Gulliford and Miller, 2015a; Reinke et al., 2011), gender and sexual diversity issues (Meyer, 2010) and critical incidents (Department for Education [Northern Ireland], 2018). This 'pastoral' role of a teacher, with its emphasis on commitment to pupils, pupil protection, pupil safety and pupil health well-being, and the nature of the special relationship between teachers and their pupils, is also at the heart of effective teaching. It is important for an understanding of teacher professional identity and taps into the 'emotional intelligence' of the teacher and 'teacher self-efficacy'.

Emotional intelligence is defined by Mayer et al. (2004, p. 197) as: 'the capacity to reason about emotions, and of emotions to enhance thinking. It includes the abilities to accurately perceive emotions, to access and generate emotions so as to assist thought, to understand emotions and emotional knowledge, and to reflectively regulate emotions so as to promote emotional and intellectual growth'. The concept subsumes self-monitoring, self-awareness and social-awareness of emotions and

Table 2.2 Responsibilities of the 'Pastoral' role

Role	Examples of Responsibilities
'Pastoral'	<ul><li>Take responsibility for promoting and safeguarding the welfare of children and young people within the school</li><li>Promote the safety and well-being of pupils in accordance with the school's safeguarding and Child Protection and other relevant policies</li><li>Be a Form Tutor to an assigned group of pupils</li><li>Encourage pupils in developing self-esteem and respect for others</li></ul>

research studies of the relationship between emotional intelligence and teacher professional identity are discussed later in this chapter.

The concept of teacher self-efficacy defined by Woolfolk Hoy (2000) as 'teachers' confidence in their ability to promote students' learning' has its origins in the work of Bandura (1977) on self-efficacy beliefs, important influences on motivation and achievement across a wide range of contexts in education, employment and well-being. Teacher self-efficacy beliefs are associated with levels of goal-setting, persistence and openness to trying new strategies and can be understood at the level both of the individual teacher and of teachers' shared values and beliefs within a school ('collective efficacy'). Teacher self-efficacy is held to have an impact upon teaching behaviour and student outcomes, with those with a strong sense of professional identity who are confident in their teaching abilities more likely to be effective and resilient teachers (Klassen et al., 2011), as we shall discuss later in this chapter.

Teaching is difficult and requires considerable subject-specific and technical knowledge. The responsibilities for the role of 'Professional Development and Training' are given in Table 2.3. These cover the expertise of the teacher and the responsibility of teachers to keep up-to-date in the curriculum developments appropriate for the sector and stages that they work in (Brownell et al., 2009), and is also identified as a key element of being an effective teacher (Kington et al., 2014). As a coda, it also defines the responsibilities of school managers to ensure that continuing professional development (CPD) opportunities reflect the needs of teachers, pupils and schools and also that training provided conforms to evidence-based approaches to effective adult learning, with opportunities for formal, informal and independent modes of learning and mentoring and coaching (Jones and Dexter, 2014; Joyce and Showers, 2002; Louws et al., 2017).

Table 2.3 Responsibilities and illustrative examples of the 'Professional Development and Training' role

Role	Examples of Responsibilities
'Professional Development and Training'	• Know subject(s) or specialism(s) to enable effective teaching • Participating in In-Service education and training courses as well as in CPD opportunities, and taking part in action research exercises • Take account of wider curriculum developments

The role of 'working with colleagues' at a practical level incorporates responsibilities for team-work and collaboration (Bates, 2019) which are given in Table 2.4. Again, these are held to be associated with effective teaching. Michael Fullan has further developed an understanding of the challenges and opportunities arising from this role by his model of 'professional accountability', which is based upon the 'professional capital of teachers' (Fullan et al., 2015). A key component of

Fullan's model which is relevant here is that of 'collective capacity and responsibility' whereby improvements in teaching and learning can result from collaboration amongst colleagues in a school, and indeed, across a network of schools, and by fostering a sense of shared responsibility or shared accountability for student learning by making good practice 'visible' (see also Hattie, 2012).

Table 2.4 Responsibilities and illustrative examples of the 'Working with Colleagues' role

Role	Examples of Responsibilities
'Working with Colleagues'	• Collaborate and work with colleagues and other relevant professionals within and beyond the school • To work effectively as a member of the school team, establishing and maintaining good relationships with colleagues, parents and pupils • Cooperate with other staff to ensure a sharing and effective usage of resources to the benefit of the school, department and pupils

It is axiomatic that teachers should be good communicators, and hence the role of 'communication' shown with associated responsibilities in Table 2.5 is also held to be central to effective teaching (Castle and Buckler, 2018; Cline, 2015; Kington et al., 2014). Communication as understood here involves communication with both pupils and parents and carers about achievement and well-being and thus has to consider the diversity of languages in the homes of many pupils and issues regarding the use of minority languages (Castells, 2010; Mohr et al., 2018).

Table 2.5 Responsibilities and illustrative examples of the 'Communication' role

Role	Examples of Responsibilities
'Communication'	• Be the first point of contact for parents of pupils • Communicate, as appropriate, with parents of pupils and persons or bodies outside the school concerned with the welfare of individual pupils, after consultation with appropriate staff • Communicate with pupils, parents and carers in accordance with the school ethos, policies and practice

The role of 'citizenship and ethos' shown in Table 2.6 considers the importance of teachers' shared goals, values and beliefs regarding the importance of mutual respect which contribute to the ethos of a school and also participation in meetings and assemblies which are held to be associated with being an effective teacher (Castle and Buckler, 2018; Cline, 2015b). The issue of values and beliefs will be considered further in the next section on the professional identity of the teacher.

Table 2.6 Responsibilities and illustrative examples of the 'Citizenship and Ethos' role

Role	Examples of Responsibilities
'Citizenship and Ethos'	• Contribute to the corporate life of the school through effective participation in meetings and systems necessary to coordinate the management of the school • Attend assemblies and actively assist in the supervision of pupils • Treat all members of the school community, colleagues and pupils, with respect and consideration

Finally, schools are organizations and, as in all organizations, there are administrative and organizational tasks and duties that have to be carried out efficiently, as shown in Table 2.7. These duties include the leadership and managerial roles of promoted staff and coordinators which will reflect priorities driven by the culture of the organization as well as national, local authority and school policies, which contribute to effective teaching (Castle and Buckler, 2018; Cline, 2015b; Teasley, 2017).

Table 2.7 Responsibilities and illustrative examples of the 'Administration' role

Role	Examples of Responsibilities
'Administration'	• Providing the necessary information and advice to the designated personnel in the school and to provide all the necessary information regarding requisitions and arrangements in connection with the teaching of the assigned subject(s) • To manage the coordination of a curriculum area or non-curriculum area • Participate in and carry out any administrative and organizational tasks within the remit of the current school teachers' conditions of service

In conclusion, thematic analysis of the job descriptions from a small convenience sample of advertised vacancies for teaching posts in England reveals that teachers have a range of wider roles and responsibilities which extend beyond teaching and learning in the classroom. These constitute the 'what' of teaching and help to define some of the characteristics of effective teaching. However, it is interesting to note that in some English schools, some year heads are not teachers, and the pastoral remit might also be undertaken by non-teachers. This raises the question of whether the outsourcing and removal of some of these roles from the remit of the teacher might have an impact upon the professional 'self'.

The thematic analysis also highlights the importance of the 'social world' of the teacher that encompasses not only the classroom and the school as an organization, but also group, societal, policy and cultural influences upon the remits and responsibilities, beliefs and values of teachers.

> **Reflective question**
> How do the roles and responsibilities reviewed here compare with those in the school(s) you are working in?

> **Reflexive question**
> How important is personal experience in the career choice to become a teacher?

Professional identity: Insights from psychological theory

Psychological theories which have been used to account for what it is to 'be' a teacher include activity theory (see Feryok, 2009), the 'Communities of Practice' framework (see Butler et al., 2004) and self-determination theory (see Ryan and Deci, 2000). Here, we will focus on contributions from role identity theory' (McCall and Simmons, 1978), social identity theory (Tajfel, 1978) and 'figured worlds' theory (Holland et al., 1998), three established and influential theoretical positions that have particular relevance for understanding teacher professional identity and that also take account of the relationship between professional identity and roles and responsibilities in the social world of schools.

Role identity theory

From the perspective of role identity theory, roles within a group or organization define identity and the theory has been used to explore the professional identity of teachers (e.g. Phillippo and Stone, 2013; Stets and Burke, 2000; Stryker and Burke, 2000).

Role identity is formed or 'activated' through 'self-verification', a reflexive cognitive process which categorizes the 'self' in terms of a role and its relationship to other roles and then in turn incorporates the meaning of this role (together with the associated norms and expectations regarding levels of performance of the role) into the self. By this means, the self is then seen in terms of this role, and role identity established.

Performance norms and expectations are important considerations in role identity theory because self-esteem (feelings of self-worth), self-efficacy (understanding and confidence in the ability to achieve goals), self-regulation (the control of behaviour and emotions to achieve those goals) and motivation are all affected by performance in the role. Individuals make 'intragroup' comparisons with others performing the same role, with a process of 'self-verification' employed to ensure that standards of behaviour are in line with the expectations of the role; favourable comparisons lead to improvements in self-esteem, self-efficacy and self-regulation, while unfavourable comparisons can have negative effects. Negotiation of normative performance standards and expectations regarding differential performance is thus an important part of role identity theory and of determining the 'meanings' of roles (Stets and Burke, 2000) and *intragroup relations* based on the different roles within a group are central to the construction of professional identity.

However, 'teacher' is not just a role, it is also a social category. From this perspective, it is possible to analyse identity at the level of *group membership*, and *intergroup relations* by means of social identity theory.

Social identity theory

Within social identity theory (Tajfel, 1978; Tajfel and Turner, 2004) the 'self' is also reflexive in that it is both 'object' and 'agent', using cognitive processes (referred to as 'tools') to construct 'social identity' based upon group membership. The theory has been widely used by researchers in studies of teacher professional identity (e.g. Barron, 2016; Black, 2008; Friesen and Besley, 2013; Stets and Burke, 2000; Stryker and Burke, 2000).

'Social identity' is a view of 'self' defined in terms of identification with a group and a sense of 'belongingness' to it (Tajfel and Turner, 2004). The cognitive process of social categorization underpins the classification and ordering of the 'social environment' and facilitates 'self-referencing' of where an individual 'fits' into society. The process of social comparison is used to label those judged to be similar to the 'self' as the 'in-group', and those categorized as different as the 'out-group'. A third cognitive tool, self-categorization, is also used to highlight similarities between the self and members of the in-group and by this means to further enhance the process of social identification. Group membership based on perceptions of social identity is then internalized as part of the individual's self-concept, for example, with those who are teachers forming an 'in-group', and those who are not teachers forming an 'out-group' (Tajfel, 1978).

Individuals' perceptions of self-worth and self-esteem are dependent upon two factors: firstly, whether social identity as defined by in-group membership is seen as positive (e.g. a source of pride and social status), rather than negative; and secondly, by the group's acceptance of the membership of the individual. The theory holds that individuals seek to realize and maintain a social identity (i.e. membership of an in-group) which is positive relative to out-groups which will increase perceptions of self-esteem and social status. However, these perceptions may be enhanced not only by feelings of pride in the standing and status of an in-group, but also by use of negative stereotyping and discrimination against out-groups. The theory describes a mechanism for this, *depersonalization* (Stets and Burke, 2000), a cognitive process which is employed after a social identity has been 'activated' (and in terms of the theory has 'salience'), whereby the individual's actions increasingly become informed by their perceptions of the norms and expectations of the in-group. This process can have positive effects by increasing cooperation, group cohesion and belongingness, but it may result in the stereotyping and prejudice noted by Tajfel (1978) in his earlier research.

'Figured worlds' theory

'Figured worlds' theory was developed by Dorothy Holland and her colleagues as part of a larger theory of self and identity, and has been used by researchers to explore the ways that individuals form or 'author' not only personal identities (e.g. taking into account life experience and the impact of culture, gender, ethnicity and social class) but also professional identity, which in the case of teachers takes into consideration the cultural and social worlds of schools and classrooms (e.g. Barron, 2016; Hsieh, 2010, 2015; Ma and Singer-Gabella, 2011; Urrieta, 2007; Varghese and Snyder, 2018).

Based upon principles drawn from Vygotsky (1978) and Bakhtin (1981), identity here is seen as being embedded in contexts shaped by social, cultural and historical ('history-in-system' at the level of the group, and 'history-in-person') influences, mediated by cultural 'tools' such as language and ways of thinking and of 'doing'.

Identity is 'figured out' (Urrieta, 2007) in a 'figured world', which is defined as:

> A socially and culturally constructed realm of interpretation in which particular characters and actors are recognised, significance is assigned to certain acts, and particular outcomes are valued over others. Each is a simplified world populated by a set of agents [...] who engage in a limited range of meaningful acts or changes of state [...] as moved by a specific set of forces.
>
> (Holland et al., 1998, p. 52)

Our identities, personal, relational and professional, across a range of contexts, are thus constructed in response to the discourse, interactions, activities and practice we experience and are exposed to in multiple 'figured worlds'. These discourses are initially the narratives of others, but in time become internalized and eventually become the narrative and discourse of the individual.

The process of 'positionality' is central to identity construction and highlights the importance of the role of 'agency', or individual choices and decision-making. 'Positions' such as student teacher, experienced teacher, competent teacher are presented to an individual by the other actors or 'social types' in a figured world. These positions can be accepted, rejected or negotiated by the individual, in what Holland and colleagues refer to as a 'space of authoring'.

The professional identity of a teacher, of what it is to 'be' a teacher and of how the individual defines and understands themselves to be a teacher, is constructed or 'self-authored' in work-related 'figured worlds' through negotiation of the multiple role-related discourses, dialogues or narratives which the individual is exposed to from experiences of different approaches to teaching and from participation in activities in the social and cultural worlds of teaching. Each different experience might constitute an alternative figured world, with professional identity constructed from multiple figured models of teaching over time. There may also be a social rank or power dynamic, with some discourses regarded as more authoritative and carrying more weight for the individual if they are the views of those of higher status within the teaching profession.

Within figured worlds, individuals can value certain activities and outcomes over others which reflects beliefs, motivation and emotional attachment to 'being' a teacher. Over the course of a teaching career, therefore, there could be a series of multiple figured worlds for the development of teacher professional identity; one for a student teacher in training; another for a beginning teacher in the early stages of her career; and yet another for a more experienced teacher. For a detailed example of the construction and negotiation of the professional identity of three beginning teachers highlighting the contributions of experience before becoming a teacher, experiences in the classroom and the intersectionality of multiple discourses, see Hsieh (2015).

Discussion

To summarize, each of the three theories reviewed here accounts for the relationships between roles, responsibilities and related expectations and professional identity. However, they offer distinctive understandings. Role identity can be characterized as a theory of 'doing', where teacher identity and its meaning are defined by the intragroup performance expectations of the roles and responsibilities of the teacher as defined within the school organization, while in contrast, social identity theory is a theory of 'being', with identity based upon uniformity and consensus of shared beliefs, values, opinions and behaviour defined by in-group membership and intergroup comparisons (Stets and Burke, 2000). 'Figured worlds' theory, on the other hand, places more emphasis upon the details of the processes underlying the social construction of professional identity and upon the importance of discourse and narrative and of negotiation for self-authoring identity. But what of the research literature? What do empirical studies tell us about teacher professional identity and the professional 'self', the sense of 'self' as a teacher?

> **Reflective question**
> How useful are psychological theories of professional identity for teachers?

> **Reflexive questions**
> 1. How important is the sense of belonging to a 'community' with colleagues in your school?
> 2. Does this affect your understanding of your professional identity as a teacher?

Research on teacher professional identity

Large-scale cross-sectional surveys (where data are collected at one time-point), longitudinal surveys (where data are collected over consecutive time-points, allowing investigation of causality) and smaller scale case studies of teachers' discourse and narrative from around the world have been used to investigate the following key research questions:

What is the nature of teacher professional identity?

Studies indicate that 'teacher professional identity' is fluid, developing over time (Beijaard et al., 2004; Day et al., 2006). It is also multifaceted in character, with interrelated underlying dimensions such as self-image, teacher self-efficacy, self-esteem, motivation, and perceptions of the role(s) of the teacher both as they are at present and may develop in the future. These are allied to knowledge and beliefs linked to the individual's reflections on their experience of teaching (and of being taught) and also to personal values (see Beijaard et al., 2004; Canrinus et al., 2011; Hong, 2010; Kelchtermans, 1993).

How does professional identity develop over the course of pre-service training and a teaching career? Does teacher education play a part in the formation of professional identity?

Turning to the formation and development of professional identity in beginning, pre-service teachers, findings indicate that individuals choose a career in teaching with expectations based upon their own personal, autobiographical experience and values (Casteneda, 2011; Friesen and Besley, 2013; Hong, 2010; Varghese and Snyder, 2018) and then 'construct, deconstruct and reconstruct' teacher professional identity (Barron, 2016) through practical experiences on block teaching placements or practicums. These experiences of teaching practice in classrooms provide opportunities to develop not only classroom skills, pedagogical and subject knowledge, but also teacher self-efficacy; a sense of 'voice'; agency; and a 'vision' of what it is to 'be' a teacher, achieved with the support of mentors and experienced colleagues (Casteneda, 2011; Conderman and Johnston-Rodriguez, 2009; Harlow and Cobb, 2014; Izadinia, 2016; Lamote and Engels, 2010; Woolfolk Hoy, 2000). Teacher education provides opportunities for learning about new ideas and pedagogical approaches and while there may be tensions between theory and practice ('theory-practice dissonance'), beginning teachers value opportunities to try out ideas and approaches in practice with support from their mentors, lecturers and tutors (Barron, 2016; Ruohotie-Lyhty and Moate, 2016; Timoštšuk and Ugaste, 2010). Studies highlight the importance of growth in confidence and teacher self-efficacy over pre-service training which is associated with involvement in the practice of teaching and in the school community via engagement with students, teacher colleagues and school leadership alike and also to low 'burn-out' rates and high levels of remaining in the profession (Harlow and Cobb, 2014; Izadinia, 2016; Kanadlı, 2017; Lamote and Engels, 2010). Finally, beginning teachers express concern about the challenging context of teaching, particularly time demands and an emphasis upon administration, and 'standards' and outcomes and delivery of content at the perceived expense of pupil-centred and flexible and creative teaching (Barron, 2016; Chong et al., 2011; Lamote and Engels, 2010).

Does professional identity have an impact upon the motivation and commitment of teachers?

A large-scale survey of 1,214 secondary school teachers in the Netherlands explored the relationships between dimensions of professional identity such as teacher self-efficacy, motivation, satisfaction with the job and commitment to being a teacher (Canrinus et al., 2011). The findings revealed that teacher self-efficacy (the individual's feelings of competence as a teacher in the classroom setting) and quality of relationships with colleagues were the strongest influences upon motivation and commitment for beginning, experienced and senior teachers. Other large-scale studies also report links between motivation and factors such as self-esteem, well-being and resilience, emotional intelligence and organizational and management processes in the school (Akar and Üstüner, 2017; Alam and Ahmad, 2018; Cordingley et al., 2019; Hong, 2010; Mocanu and Sterian, 2013; Sammons et al., 2007).

Does 'belonging' to a community of teachers impact upon professional identity?

Research indicates that the participation, feedback (both positive and negative), collaborative interactions and support from mentors, colleagues and school leadership which are part of 'belonging' to the culture of a community of teachers are fundamental to constructing and re-constructing professional identity over the course of a teaching career (Casteneda, 2011; Conderman and Johnston-Rodriguez, 2009; Darby, 2008; Sammons et al., 2007; Steyn, 2018).

Do understandings of teacher professional identity differ between countries and educational jurisdictions?

This issue is considered in more detail in the case study, with reference to the survey and interviews carried out by Cordingley et al. (2019). The findings from the study confirm contextual and individual differences between the seven countries taking part but also marked consensus concerning the importance for professional identity of roles and expectations, professional development and relationships, and concern for student well-being and achievement.

Case study: Cordingley et al. (2019) 'Constructing Teachers' Professional Identities'

Countries: Canada, Scotland (UK), Singapore, Sweden, Germany, Chile and Kenya

Age group: Adults (teachers) responsible for teaching pupils from Years 1 to 12 in the age range of 5–17 years

Setting: Schools based together with follow-up interviews involving policymakers

Participants: 4,850 teachers and policymakers from schools in North America, South America, Europe, Asia and Africa

Case study: The International Teacher Professional Identity Survey was informed by an earlier systematic literature review with the aim of investigating the construction of teachers' professional identities. To take into account effects of economic and geographical variables on teacher identity, seven different education systems from around the world were chosen to reflect a range of different pupil performance outcomes, staffing and employment conditions and a sample of teachers from each jurisdiction invited to complete a specially designed survey questionnaire to find out about the effects on teacher professional identity of policies relating to classroom practices, professional learning and development, regulation and qualification, systems for accountability, teacher voice and leadership, and social and cultural contexts. The questionnaire data were further supported by follow-up semi-structured interviews, focus group interviews and more detailed case studies.

Outcomes: Response rates varied markedly, with returns from teachers in Canada and Scotland combined accounting for 71 per cent of the total, while Chile, with a significantly shorter time for responding than the other countries, had the lowest response rate, accounting for only 1 per cent, so caution is required in the interpretation of the results.

The findings revealed that while there were significant individual and contextual differences and challenges, teachers in the main regarded professional self-development as central to their professional identity, and took a holistic approach, regarding the quality of teaching, learning and the well-being of their pupils as paramount, even to the detriment of work–life balance. Teacher status, opportunities for professional development, and opportunities for promotion and advancement within the profession were all associated with levels of performance of the education system. Working conditions, status and salaries also had a significant impact upon the supply of teachers across the seven countries.

What can we learn? Despite diversity and many economic challenges in some of the jurisdictions, there are marked communalities across participants from the seven countries involved in the survey and follow-up data collection. The study confirmed the centrality of roles and expectations, of professional relationships and networks, of collaboration with teacher colleagues, and also of a sense of self-efficacy and agency on the part of individual teachers.

Does professional identity make a difference to how teachers 'teach' and to the effectiveness of their teaching?

A direct link between teacher personal identity and effective teaching is difficult to establish as in addition to problems of definition and measurement of such a complex construct as 'professional identity' (Beijaard et al., 2004; Day et al., 2006; Klassen et al., 2011), most research studies utilize cross-sectional designs which cannot 'prove' causal relationships. However, a recent systematic review by Zee and Koomen (2016) of the impact of teacher self-efficacy from 165 papers across forty years revealed positive associations between measures of the teachers' self-efficacy and their psychological well-being. There were associations between teacher self-efficacy and the quality of classroom practices and the pupils' academic adjustment. But the findings regarding teacher self-efficacy and pupil achievement were less clear-cut. The review identified twenty-two studies of the impact upon pupil achievement, but the authors were unable to synthesize the outcomes for pupil achievement as the data would not permit a meta-analysis.

However, Sammons and colleagues (2007) carried out a large-scale prospective longitudinal study of 300 teachers in England over three academic sessions and found that aspects of teacher professional identity, particularly commitment, motivation and resilience, did make a significant difference to the effectiveness of teaching and to the students' attainments, accounting for some 15–30 per cent in pupil academic outcomes in Years 6 and 9, that is pupils aged between 12 and 16 years. Further, Summers and colleagues (2017) in a large-scale prospective follow-up study in the United States found that teachers' self-efficacy beliefs were predictive of the quality of teacher–pupil relationships, with more confident teachers with higher expectations having better relationships and less conflict. Finally, turning to emotional intelligence, Alam and Ahmad (2018) carried out a large-scale study of 224 teachers in Pakistan which revealed a complex relationship between teachers' emotional intelligence and pupil outcomes which was mediated by the effects of school culture, highlighting again the importance of context.

Discussion

These research studies provide important insights into the nature and impact of teacher professional identity and its construction. However, it is important to note a lack of consistency in the definitions of professional identity used by researchers and the representativeness of the samples of participants, particularly in the case of the small-scale case studies (Beijaard et al., 2004) and problems of response rates in follow-up data collection in longitudinal studies (Sammons et al., 2007). There are also issues regarding the reliability and validity of measurement of teacher professional identity which are considered in more detail in the Window on research. And while small-scale studies of teacher narratives informed by social identity and 'figured worlds' theories have helped to illuminate the complexity of the construct of 'teacher professional identity' and its formation, there is also a need for more large-scale prospective cohort studies to address the relationship between professional identity and student outcomes across different age groups and subject areas.

Window on research

Lentillon-Kaestner et al. (2018). 'Validity and reliability of questionnaire on perceived professional identity among teachers (QIPPE) scores', *Studies in Educational Evaluation*, 59, pp. 235–43. Doi: 10.1016/j.stueduc.2018.09.003

Countries: France and Switzerland

Age group: Adults (teachers)

Setting: Schools

Participants involved: Study 1: a first sample of 205 experienced teachers responsible for teaching secondary school-age pupils in schools in France and a second sample of 350 experienced French secondary school teachers; and Study 2: 194 experienced secondary school teachers in Switzerland.

Aim: This study was designed to address the lack of reliable and valid instruments to measure teacher professional identity by developing an instrument for use in research in this area. The instrument was based upon the authors' choice of 'expertise' as an appropriate measure of teacher professional identity.

Outcomes: In Study 1, a twenty-seven-item questionnaire was first administered online to 205 participants. Preliminary statistical analysis revealed that sixteen of the twenty-seven items performed poorly, yielding an eleven-item final scale consisting of three underlying 'factors', corresponding to the dimensions of teacher professional identity: didactical expertise, pedagogical expertise and subject matter expertise. A further psychometric analysis indicated that these factors were measured reliably. The eleven-item final scale was then administered to a second independent sample of 350 teachers, but here, a simpler factor structure of pedagogical expertise and subject matter expertise was observed. Analysis confirmed the reliability of these two factors. In Study 2, the validity of the two-factor eleven-item instrument was determined by comparing scores from the three underlying factors with scores from the nineteen-item Multidimensional Work Motivation Scale. Scores for pedagogical expertise and subject matter expertise were correlated with scores for motivation, although the levels of correlation are modest.

What we can learn: This paper, although technical, illustrates the process of meeting the need for a reliable and valid measure of teacher professional identity which could be used in research. The dimensions of teacher professional identity measured by the scale, pedagogical expertise and subject matter expertise, and their links with motivation have been confirmed by other research studies, some of which are discussed in this chapter. However, although the scale is a reliable measure, it remains somewhat limited, with its narrow focus upon teacher professional identity as 'expertise'. While the authors provide a rationale for this, the modest levels of the correlations between the two measures of expertise and the measures of motivation reported highlight the need for a measure of teacher professional identity which captures its multidimensional nature, perhaps by the incorporation of additional items which tap into self-efficacy and strength of relationships with mentors and colleagues.

Conclusion

In this chapter, the relationship between the 'personal' and 'professional self', and identity and teacher professional identity in the light of the roles, responsibilities and expectations of 'being' a teacher have been considered. The complexity of the construct and its formation and development in the light of three theories of teacher professional identity, role identity theory, social identity theory and 'figured worlds' theory and in the light of research have also been discussed.

Key understandings are that teacher professional identity is socially constructed through narratives and discourse and experience of teaching in the social world of schools, in the light of personal history and values, roles and expectations of 'doing the job'; that it is fluid and develops by processes of construction and reconstruction over the course of training and a career through feedback and negotiation; and the importance of self-efficacy and relationships with mentors, colleagues and school leaders for the effectiveness of teaching, job satisfaction, well-being, motivation and commitment to the teaching profession.

Reflective questions

1. How might removing the remit for a role such as pastoral support from a teacher's responsibilities in a school impact upon their sense of professional identity?
2. How might you provide support and mentoring to a less experienced colleague?

> **Reflexive questions**
>
> 1. Does your understanding of teacher professional identity differ from that of colleagues from different disciplines? To what extent might subject area or stage of pupils taught make a difference?
> 2. Have there been any changes in your own professional identity as a teacher over the course of pre-service training or your career? If so, what might have contributed to these?

Implications for Teachers

- Responsibilities and expectations regarding teaching, pastoral, professional development and training, collaborative, communication, citizenship and administrative roles help to define the 'what' of teaching.
- An understanding of teacher professional identity helps to define what it 'is' to be a teacher.
- Practical experience in schools and classrooms is crucial to the construction and development of teacher professional identity.
- Teaching is a challenging context and mentoring, collaboration and support from colleagues and school leaders and management and positive relationships helps in the ongoing development of teacher professional development over a career by fostering a sense of 'belonging'.
- Development of subject expertise, classroom skills and pedagogical knowledge in a supportive workplace setting underpin growth of confidence, and a sense of agency and self-efficacy, which are important for successful engagement with pupils, job satisfaction and well-being.

Annotated bibliography

Barron, I. (2016). 'Flight turbulence: The stormy professional trajectory of trainee early years' teachers in England', *International Journal of Early Years Education*, 24(3), pp. 325–41. doi:10.1080/09669760.2016.1204906.
A study of the development of professional identity through the lens of 'figured worlds'.

Canrinus, E. T., Helms-Lorenz, M., Beijaard, D., Buitink, J. and Hofman, A. (2011). 'Self-efficacy, job satisfaction, motivation and commitment: Exploring the relationships between indicators of teachers' professional identity', *European Journal of Psychology of Education*, 27(1), pp. 115–32. doi:10.1007/s10212-011-0069-2.

A large-scale study which explores the relationships between key factors underpinning the concept of teacher professional identity.

Sammons, P., Day, C., Kington, A., Gu, Q., Stobart, G. and Smees, R. (2007). 'Exploring variations in teachers' work, lives and their effects on pupils: Key findings and implications from a longitudinal mixed method study', *British Educational Research Journal,* **33(5), pp. 681–701. doi:10.1080/01411920701582264.**

A large-scale longitudinal study of the relationship between teachers' well-being and professional identity and pupil outcomes.

3
Health and Well-Being in Psychology
Lisa Marks Woolfson and Stuart Woodcock

It is widely recognized that teaching is both a valuable and a challenging job. The profession attracts idealistic people who want to make a difference to children and young people's lives. Worrying statistics of 30–50 per cent dropout in the first few years of teaching have been reported (e.g. Izadinia, 2015). In this chapter we discuss some of the important factors that can facilitate new teachers settling into and adjusting to their new professional role by developing the necessary psychosocial attributes that will help them. We draw upon literature from the areas of work and health psychology for this and consider their application to education and the work of new teachers in the school as an organization.

Well-being

While there is no shortage of talk about well-being on social media, television, newspapers, magazines and popular culture generally, the concept is often used with a rather vague meaning. Let's clarify what we mean by 'well-being' in this chapter. As long ago as 1948, the World Health Organization defined 'health' as more than not having a disease, recognizing rather it encompasses psychological and mental health and social well-being too. It is those psychological, personal, social and emotional aspects of well-being that this chapter will focus upon, when it refers to well-being.

Well-being at work is recognized as a key issue for organizations, for individuals and for the wider society. It is further understood that work and well-being are linked to each other in complex ways and that each can impact on the other. Teaching as a profession presents particular and unique challenges. In February 2019 the United Kingdom National Foundation for Educational Research reported that 20 per cent of teachers felt tense about their job all or most of the time, compared to 13 per cent carrying out similar types of jobs, such as health professionals, engineers, scientists,

IT professionals, lawyers, social workers and librarians. It is clear that we need to be thinking about how to enhance teacher mental health and well-being.

Window on research

Researching psychological well-being

There are two major ways in which research conceptualizes psychological well-being (Royer and Moreau, 2016). Firstly, it can be characterized as a subjective notion. You enjoy your work, you like being a teacher. You experience more positive than negative emotions around your work activities, according to your own subjective judgement and standards. This notion of well-being at work as job satisfaction is referred to as the 'hedonic' perspective.

But well-being at work can likewise be considered from a psychological viewpoint as providing a context for fulfilment of personal meaning and purpose, for competence and mastery of teaching and interpersonal skills, allowing you to accomplish goals and experience greater autonomy. This conceptualization of well-being is focused on growth, both personal and professional, across a range of dimensions. This is referred to as the 'eudaimonic' perspective.

Well-being in the workplace can be viewed as achieving an acceptable balance between the demands of the work environment on the one hand, and a person's goals, needs and expectations in that job, on the other. So it is typically measured by individual self-report questionnaires on stress and burnout, on job satisfaction and on self-efficacy (e.g. Naghieh et al., 2015). Typical stress and burnout items are 'I am under pressure with a heavy workload', 'problems at school make me bad-tempered with family and friends', ' I often need to take work home'. Examples of job satisfaction items include 'I enjoy teaching', 'I like the other staff I work with', 'I feel appreciated when I do a good job'. Teacher self-efficacy can be measured with items like 'I am confident that I can respond to difficult behaviour in the classroom', 'I can adapt the curriculum for students who are struggling', 'I can use a variety of assessment strategies'.

Well-being research aims to answer questions about antecedent factors that contribute to staff well-being at work, and outcomes of workplace interventions to improve well-being. For example, Jennings and DeMauro (2017) examined how well mindfulness interventions help in reducing teacher stress and burnout in the workplace, reporting a growing evidence base for positive effects on well-being.

Organizations measure well-being indirectly by using proxy indicators such as staff sickness absence and staff turnover. Organizational dimensions such as management style, health and safety practices, physical environment and organizational support systems influence well-being in the workplace. Such organizational dimensions though are beyond the reach of many teachers to address so in this chapter we examine only psychosocial dimensions that influence well-being at work, that are within the control of the individual to take action on, and that have practical implications for your well-being as a teacher.

Social identity

As a teacher, you have a socially constructed role which is laid out for you. Instead of being part of the social group of 'students' or 'teachers-in-training', you are a member of the social group, 'teachers'. Perceiving yourself as belonging to a social group is recognized as important by social psychologists. This is because categorizing oneself as a member of a group confers upon its members a commitment to a particular social identity that influences their attitudes, beliefs and values. As well as this, there is an evaluative component where you decide whether belonging to this group is a good thing or not (e.g. Bergami and Bagozzi, 2000). So while you see yourself as belonging to the group of teachers at a particular school, you may, for example, evaluate being a teacher at another school as being better, because you've heard the school principal there is more sympathetic and supportive to the needs of new staff. Or you may be aware that the school has a poor reputation for student learning and behaviour or a disgruntled, unsupportive group of colleagues. You may then identify less strongly with the social group 'teachers at that school' and feel less emotionally attached to this group and to your work there and less committed and engaged with the goals and aspirations of that school. On the other hand, you may take on the values of the school you are in and become disgruntled like the rest of this social group. Note though that identity is dynamic and changes over time. Your view of your professional identity and sub-identities within this will change as you gain experience, and through your work in different schools with different colleagues, managers, climates and values. Initially your experiences in teaching practice and in the teacher education programme will shape your professional identity. The school context in which you work will continue to develop it.

Beauchamp and Thomas (2009) explain an important link between identity and agency. Agency is the power to act to take things forward in your professional development to reach goals, to transform your classroom into what you see as an optimal learning environment for your students, even to have an effect on school-wide policies and practices. Your view of your professional identity will influence your actions as a professional, what you do and what you think you are capable of doing. We will explore this last issue of your views of your own capability further when we consider teacher self-efficacy later in the chapter.

> **Reflexive question**
>
> What groups and subgroups do you see yourself as belonging to, as a teacher?

> **Window on research**
>
> *Social identity theory*
>
> The study of social groups has been of great interest to psychologists in terms of how groups are formed, and how they influence members' opinions and their personal identity. Groups had been viewed as people who shared personal interests and views and were therefore biased towards their group and against other groups. In the 1970s Henri Tajfel and colleagues developed social identity theory to explain the contribution that the groups people belong to make to a person's identity (Tajfel et al., 1971). Surprisingly they showed that only minimal conditions were needed for people to perceive themselves as being part of a group and therefore to be biased towards that group. It was not necessary to share personal interests at all.
>
> Tajfel found that categorization into groups could be spurious, even based on a coin toss. It seems that even just allocating a person to a group artificially in a lab situation and making this group compete with another group was sufficient to make people feel committed and biased in favour of their own group, the 'in-group'. In Tajfel's minimal group paradigm there was not even any interaction between group members. You just knew what group you had been allocated to, not who else was in your group or in the other group.
>
> Tajfel and his colleagues carried out a number of classic studies. In one study for example, participants estimated the number of dots on a screen and were then randomly divided into four groups, over-estimators, under-estimators, accurate and inaccurate. Note that these groups did not relate to participants' actual performance in estimating the dots. Participants could then allocate cash rewards based on group membership. Results showed that in allocating the rewards, people favoured the members of their own group – in-group favouritism.
>
> As well as studying intergroup relations by randomly allocating people to groups, the influence of social groups has been examined by studying pre-existing naturally occurring groups, such as minority ethnic groups, or gender-based groups. Our perception of social identity can be positive, neutral or negative depending on how we view our group in social comparison to other groups.
>
> There has though been less social identity research on work groups (e.g. Bergami and Bagozzi, 2000) and indeed specifically on the topic we are interested in, teachers in their workplaces.

You are likely to see yourself as belonging to a wider social group beyond your school, the universal professional group called teachers.

What is a teacher? What do we understand about this social group? A teacher is of course someone who has the particular set of skills, knowledge and abilities that they have developed through training and experience, and that are recognized by the teaching profession as central to the role. These include, for example, knowledge of relevant curriculum, child development, classroom management skills, classroom organization, understanding how children learn and develop literacy and numeracy skills. These may be viewed as the professional building blocks of teaching and you require knowledge of these to be effective in your day-to-day work. Their specifics may differ depending on whether you're a primary/grade school teacher or a high school teacher.

In addition to these, and just as important, there are 'soft' skills which tend to be more psychosocial in nature. There are personal skills and beliefs that relate to engaging with the values, culture and ethos of the school you're working in. They are the values that you hold and the understandings that you share with your colleagues in the teaching community. This new identity is shaped by your training, by your own values and by your working environment. For new teachers this environment is the school community for their first post. As new teachers are in the very early stages of forging their professional identity, the influence of this first school may be particularly strong. New teachers should be aware of this effect and factor this into their choice of first job, if at all possible.

A teacher's professional identity involves emotional engagement with the role and caring at an individual level (e.g. O'Connor, 2008). Shortcomings in the development of 'hard' and 'soft' skills as well as maintaining congruence between your activities and behaviours in school and your beliefs and feelings about yourself as a person and yourself as a teacher are all factors that can influence your well-being and mental health and your effectiveness as a teacher.

Role ambiguity and role conflict

What happens if there is a conflict between your values and some aspect of your professional role? The expectations teachers had when they were training may be challenged in their first year of teaching, and perhaps their ideals and values thoroughly shaken (e.g. Dicke et al., 2015). The role may be confusing with different people, children, young people, colleagues, friends, family, expecting different things from the teacher in terms of how they behave, what outcomes they can achieve, what their priorities are or indeed what they think about educational matters.

Schwab and Iwanicki (1982) investigated role conflict by asking teachers about when they were asked to do things that they felt should be done differently, or to undertake tasks without sufficient resources, or where teachers were unclear what their role was in a particular activity, what was expected of them or what their responsibilities were. Role conflict and role ambiguity have been recognized by researchers as potential sources of stress, and found to influence teacher satisfaction and to be related to emotional exhaustion and burnout (e.g. Danna and Griffin, 1999; Schwab and Iwanicki, 1982) of which more later.

Genuineness in your role

Carl Rogers (1902–87) was an influential psychologist who was one of the founders of 'humanistic psychology'. His focus was on counselling adults to help them solve their life problems, but his approach has important implications for teacher–pupil relationships and in particular the teacher role. Rogers viewed what he called 'realness' or 'genuineness', as a key teacher quality for facilitating learning, similarly to how he viewed it as a core condition for effective client–counsellor relationships (e.g. Rogers, 2002). This is where the teacher is present in the classroom as an authentic person in their relationships with their students, showing their human self, rather than a false front. Integrating personal and professional aspects is a key challenge in the development of your identity as a teacher (e.g. Beijaard, Meijer and Verloop, 2004).

> **Reflective question**
>
> How can a teacher be authentic in the classroom yet still adhere to personal and professional boundaries?

One way of thinking about this is that 'teacher' is not the only role you have in life. Your professional role intersects with, for example, gender, ethnicity, religion, sexuality, disability and politics. So alongside being a teacher in your classroom, you have other roles within other communities outside that of the school, for example, as a child and/or parent within a non-traditional family, as a gay person, a member of a religious community, a musician in a band. How much of yourself can you then share without sharing too much of your personal life or even being viewed as influencing children and young people towards your own lifestyle choices? How 'real' can you be with your students?

Case study: Newly qualified teachers understanding boundaries

Country: Australia

Age group: Primary/Elementary School

Setting: Reidtown Public School is a government coeducation primary school (Kindergarten–Year 6) in regional New South Wales. There are approximately 450 pupils enrolled with an age range of 5–12 years.

Participants involved: Mr Clarke is a 24-year-old male primary school teacher. He is currently teaching Year 5 students aged 10–11 years.

Case study: Mr Clarke is a primary school teacher who completed his Master of Teaching (teacher training) course 2 years ago. Mr Clarke is gay and on 9 December 2017, when same-sex marriage became legal in Australia, he married his partner. He is a vocal advocate for the LGBTQI (lesbian, gay, bisexual, transgender [transsexual], queer [questioning] and intersex) community and has participated in the Sydney Gay and Lesbian Mardi Gras for the past seven years. During class Mr Clarke often gives personal examples to illustrate the point he is teaching as he feels that brings the topic to life, helps understanding and can build a positive rapport in the classroom. He often talks about his husband who is also a teacher. He has occasionally talked about issues that concern the LGBTQI community, such as experience of discrimination in the workplace or bullying at school. He believes that it is important for children and young people to understand about diversity and inclusion.

Outcomes: A group of parents have complained to the school principal that they were not happy about Mr Clarke 'introducing their children to homosexuality'. They were clear that they had 'nothing against homosexuals as such' but were concerned that Mr Clarke had disclosed that he and his husband were having relationship issues. They felt this was inappropriate and had upset some of their children who liked Mr Clarke. Some parents also mentioned that they were unhappy about discussing LGBTQI issues in class. A few felt that he was trying to 'brainwash' their children.

What can we learn? While it is not against the New South Wales *Code of Conduct* (2014) to share personal information with pupils per se, Mr Clarke was perceived by some parents as pushing boundaries. For example, a teacher can be in breach of this code of conduct if they are conversing about personal matters that are unrelated to the curriculum. According to the NSW Department of Education and Training, like many other education departments, all teachers have a number of responsibilities to carry out the high standards of professional and ethical behaviour required by the education department, the parents, the public and the profession itself. One of those responsibilities is understanding the boundaries as a teacher and duty of care towards pupils.

There is of course a limit to how much personal information to share, and the way in which you share it.

Mr Clarke was trying to be open and share part of his life to build a good rapport with the class as well as have them better understand about inclusion and diversity within society. When considering whether to share personal information to children and young people a teacher should consider the following factors: the age of the class, type of information shared and motivation for sharing the information.

Information shared needs to be *age appropriate*, as well as relevant to the class for learning purposes, as outlined in the *Code of Conduct*. It is important to think very carefully about personal boundaries and when 'sharing' may be viewed as 'influencing', even if that is not your intention.

The *type of information shared* needs to be considered. Often teachers connect with their pupils via sharing some basic information, such as their pets, or their children's names. These can often help teacher–student relationships in the classroom and support the teaching and learning to occur. However, other types of personal information can break the rules of *duty of care* if they do not consider the physical and emotional safety of the teacher and pupils in the classroom.

Sharing basic information about one's sexuality in the way Mr Clarke did by mentioning his husband would not then normally be viewed as breaking the rules of duty of care. Mr Clarke's class was comprised of 10–11-year-olds whom he judged to be mature enough to be exposed to the multiple viewpoints and different kinds of relationships that the LGBTQI community encompasses. It is important for children to learn to respect and value diversity.

Teachers' motivation for sharing information also needs to be considered. For example, the teacher may share information about her family pet. This is good use of personal information. It establishes the teacher as a person with personal values of caring and nurturing and has an educational purpose for the children as well as helping build a positive working relationship with the students in the classroom. Another reason though may include the teacher's need to talk about themselves in order to cope with a personal situation or to help relieve their own stresses and anxieties. These reasons are for the benefit of the teacher rather than the students, and the teacher is taking advantage of having a 'captive' audience. While this might show the class the teacher as a 'real' person, this type of sharing does not belong in the classroom.

Finally, and importantly it is important to recognize that sharing personal information is not the only way for a teacher to demonstrate genuineness. Teachers can share their thoughts and values with the class in relation to the children's behaviour and learning for example. They can share their feelings about class activities and admit mistakes. These teacher behaviours all indicate the teacher as a real person.

> **Reflective question**
> How do the students in your classroom know you are 'genuine'?

Autonomy

Autonomy is the extent to which you feel you have personal control in the workplace, freedom and professional independence in your work. Workplace autonomy is an important concept to be aware of as it is thought to be related to factors such as motivation and performance, job satisfaction, absenteeism, stress and burnout (e.g. Pearson and Moomaw, 2006; Spector, 1986).

It has been suggested that there are two aspects to autonomy at work: (1) control over your schedule, timing and the physical location of where you carry out your work; and (2) control over the work tasks and activities themselves (Wheatley, 2017). Class teachers have limited flexibility in terms of when and where they work as the location of teaching largely takes place within the school premises and within the hours designated by the local school board. Wheatley's study was based on analysing UK panel data from the Understand Society dataset.[1] The data they made use of did not specifically identify teachers, but rather 'professionals' as a group. It found that professional women in particular, reported less autonomy than did other groups of employees.

Having said that though, within school and classroom environmental constraints, there are still opportunities for teachers to exercise autonomy over their own classroom activities, and for their professional opinions about teaching methods to be listened to, the second aspect of autonomy outlined above. Indeed, this freedom to make judgements about what is best for those whose education is in your hands may be viewed as a key marker of professionalism. Probationary periods and supervision though can mean that new teachers feel they have less autonomy in their classrooms than their more experienced colleagues. Moreover, there is the wider concern that as curricular content and methods become more proscribed in many countries, and teachers more accountable, alongside this there may be less professional independence to make teaching decisions in the classroom, and therefore less autonomy (e.g. Pitt and Phelan, 2008).

---

[1] Understanding Society is a longitudinal UK study of households which asks questions about health and well-being and employment, as well as other topics of social and economic interest.

> **Reflexive question**
> To what extent do you feel you have control over your classroom, class timetable and your own timetable, content and delivery of your lessons?

> **Reflective question**
> If a teacher had pedagogic reasons for wanting to introduce a topic that was not currently part of the school curriculum, how could they go about gaining approval for this?

Stress, mental health and burnout

Teaching is consistently recognized as a stressful job. Recent data from both the UK Health and Safety Executive and an Australian study from Bond University show that it is indeed one of the *most* stressful jobs, with work-related stress a significant problem. Kyriacou (2001) defined teacher stress as the experience of negative emotions as a result of their work as a teacher challenging their self-esteem or well-being. Emotions experienced include anger, fear, depression, tension and anxiety (e.g. Papastylianou, Kaila and Polychronopoulos, 2009). Sources of classroom stress include managing difficult behaviour; teaching students who seem uninterested and unmotivated; large class sizes; coping with policy change; managing workload; lesson preparation and marking; administration demands; job conditions; limited resourcing; relationships with colleagues; relationships with parents; lack of support; accountability for poor student performance; lack of autonomy in what and how to teach.

Burnout may be viewed as prolonged exposure to stress at work, where the individual feels consistently stretched trying to meet job demands, or indeed that the job requires more than the individual can provide. It has been characterized as a lack of coping with stress, resulting in a kind of exhaustion that involves loss of motivation and commitment and depletion of an individual's psychological, physiological and emotional resources (e.g. Marek, Schaufeli and Maslach, 2017).

> ### Case study: Teachers handling stress and burnout
> **Country:** England
>
> **Age group:** Secondary School
>
> **Setting:** Rustington Secondary School is a coeducation community school and sixth form (years 7–13) in West Sussex. There are approximately 1,500 students enrolled with an age range of 11–18 years.

Participants involved: Mrs Lang is a 25-year-old female science teacher who is married with a three-year-old child.

Case study: Mrs Lang is a secondary science teacher who completed her Post Graduate Certificate in Education teacher training course mid-way through last year. She was looking forward to the job as well as being able to spend time with her family. In September when the new academic year began there were no job opportunities as a secondary science teacher. However, she was offered a position as a maths and science teacher. Mrs Lang hit the ground running, full of optimism, but soon began to struggle. She found it particularly challenging to apply differentiation to her teaching to meet the needs of all of her students and keeping them all engaged. She was up late every night and then up early to plan and get organized for her lessons. Preparation was taking an average of two hours for each lesson and she was teaching twenty-two lessons per week. Adding marking and other teaching duties to her already-full schedule meant that Mrs Lang was working long days, starting early, staying at school until late, going home and having dinner, starting work again and working until late into the night just to get by. This was not sustainable. Eventually she was physically exhausted and was experiencing panic attacks. By the end of the first term Mrs Lang knew that she couldn't continue like this.

She knew that she could get support from colleagues for aspects of work such as lesson plans, resources. However, she also viewed teaching as a skill and felt that managing the class and responding appropriately and effectively to students were something she should know how to do from her training, so was reluctant to ask for help.

Outcomes: While Mrs Lang was trying to be as organized as possible for each lesson that she taught, especially since maths was not her strength, she became physically exhausted which was impacting upon not only her teaching but also her home life and her health. Quality time with her husband and young child was in jeopardy.

What can we learn? There are a number of steps that can be taken to help relieve some of the stress and exhaustion and prevent burning out at any point in your teaching career, especially in the beginning stages.

(1) Ask colleagues for support and advice. It's OK not to be perfect at the job. If you prefer not to do this at the school where you work, then talk to teaching colleagues from other schools, or your beginning teacher peer group. They are probably experiencing the same problems. You can also network with others online. There are many great online forums for teachers to share resources and support one another. Teaching can be a very isolating job if you let it, but teachers can be very supportive to one another if you are open to this. Friends and family can help too. Often someone outside your role sees the way round workplace issues more clearly.

> (2) Keep tight control on how much work you take home. Family and home life are an important aspect of your overall well-being. It is necessary to prioritize what is important, rather than to be driven by demands.
>
> (3) Unwind. Find something else you enjoy other than work. Whether it is through exercise, dinner with friends, walking the dog, cooking, playing with your child, take the time to do something that will help to refresh and recharge. Relax mind and body. Yoga and mindfulness are popular choices for this.
>
> (4) Remember why you became a teacher. The stress of the job can take over and new teachers especially can forget why they decided to become a teacher in the first place. Stay away from negativity. Remember the positives and rewards from teaching. While challenges and negative issues may emerge, through the media, staffroom gossip etc., keep yourself focused on the positive aspects of the job.

Resilience and mental health

Rather than focusing on stress and burnout, things that are going wrong in the job, a more positive view is to focus on what is going right. An important question to consider then is not what causes stress and burnout, but how do teachers adapt to and cope with stress in order to avoid burnout. Thinking about this brings us to the concept of teacher resilience, a topic that is attracting increased interest in relation to teacher mental health as well as in relation to teacher effectiveness and teacher retention (e.g. Le Cornu, 2009).

Developmental psychologists began to be interested in resilience when it was noted that children growing up in similarly adverse conditions showed quite different outcomes.

Teacher resilience is the capacity for adapting well and swiftly to stresses and difficulties in the workplace that the teacher experiences. These might be relationships with colleagues, or dealing with challenges in the classroom, problematic child behaviour, workload overload, or indeed any of the stressors described in the section above. Resilience is best considered as a dynamic process, rather than a characteristic teachers have or don't have. The resilient teacher still experiences these stresses but is able to bounce back by thinking and acting in ways that facilitate coping with these sources of stress and so preventing disturbance of their mental health and well-being.

Gu and Day (2007) studied this process by following three resilient teachers at early, mid and late career stages, over a four-year period. Each of the teachers in the study experienced pressure and stress over this period, not only at school but also in their personal lives. As mentioned previously in this chapter, because being a teacher is not the only role you hold in your life, stresses and pressures in your other roles can affect your experience of the teaching role. For example, sickness in your partner may be causing you stress and so can affect how well you cope with classroom challenges.

So how can you build resilience for teaching? Let's consider how beliefs and values can help in this.

Beliefs

Attributional beliefs

How do teachers attribute the causes of problems they experience in the classroom? Causal attributions are a set of beliefs that can be classified along three dimensions (Weiner, 1985):

1. locus of causality, the source of the attribution
2. stability, whether the cause is likely to be ongoing
3. controllability, the extent to which the teacher has control over the cause of the problem

A teacher may believe that a lesson went poorly and that this has an external locus of causality. For example, she may view the lesson problems as caused by the particular curriculum content, that she thinks is too complex or not of interest to the students. This means that she sees the cause of the problem as being outside herself and so will make little effort to address the poor lesson next time. If instead however she attributes this to an internal locus of causality such as the way she taught the curricular material, then she is more likely to be resilient to the negative experience of delivering a failed lesson as she can change this and teach the lesson differently (better) next time.

> **Reflexive questions**
>
> 1. Think about your most recent teaching. What attributions did you use to explain student difficulties?
> 2. Were these internal or external attributions?

> **Reflective question**
>
> Which of these attributions would most help you plan for new ways of supporting student learning next time?

Self-efficacy

Self-efficacy beliefs have been found to be key to resilience and to distinguish between teachers who left teaching and those who remained (e.g. Gu and Day, 2007; Hong, 2012). Self-efficacy in teaching relates to teachers' beliefs in their capacity for achieving their goals, such as delivering effective teaching instruction, solving problems in the classroom and creating a positive learning environment. It originates from Albert Bandura's social cognitive theory (Bandura, 1977). Teaching self-efficacy then relates to professional identity and feelings of competence. It has often been used in research studies as a measure of well-being at work (e.g. Naghieh et al., 2015). We will see later that it is an important factor in teacher resilience. It can also be context-specific so a teacher's feelings of self-efficacy may be increased or decreased depending on the students or class they are teaching.

The school climate contributes to self-efficacy, that is to say the values and expectations of the school as an organization, staff relationships, leadership of the school principal, all are part of the school climate and the school's ethos. Mastery experience too contributes to teacher self-efficacy. This is the success you have already achieved in your teaching. For example, if, as a new teacher, you previously achieved success in the classroom during your training experience, then you will have more positive self-efficacy beliefs as you start your first teaching position. The opposite is unfortunately the case too (e.g. Wilson, Woolfson and Durkin, 2018).

Your beliefs about your own teaching self-efficacy relate to your motivation, effort and persistence in dealing with the problems and challenges of the classroom. It will not only influence how much you persist, but even what challenges you set yourself. If your belief in your own self-efficacy is low, then it is likely that you will set yourself lower goals and targets because you don't see yourself as being able to achieve any better (e.g. Bandura, 1997; Lunenburg, 2011). Teaching efficacy can be viewed as comprised of two components. One is personal self-efficacy as described above. The second is a more general belief that teaching itself has the power to overcome external influences that children experience, that teaching can bring about change and positive educational outcomes (e.g. Brady and Woolfson, 2008).

Values

This sense of the importance of teaching and furthermore feeling it to be a personal vocation is recognized as important for teacher resilience. It relates to motivation and commitment to education, to the value of learning, to improving children's lives, to making a difference to children's futures, to contributing to society. These are of course reasons why many students decide to go into teaching in the first place. This issue of values and your role as a teacher has come up earlier in this chapter where we discussed how a new teacher's values may be challenged.

> **Reflexive question**
> What do you value in teaching? To think about this, consider what you see as important in what you do/can do as a teacher.

Conclusion

Teaching is not an easy option and can be particularly challenging in the first few years.

Indeed, there are likely to be further challenges throughout your career when adapting to new jobs in different schools, or when trying to balance professional demands with personal ones such as a new baby in the family. Building resilience and a strong role identity can help avoid the extreme impacts of stress and burnout.

Implications for educators

1. Look after yourself and your health. Become aware of what situations you find stressful as a teacher and identify ways of managing and reducing stress that work for you when you find yourself in these situations. Be aware too of the antecedents of these stressful situations so that you can either avoid them or plan and prepare better for dealing with them. Stress reduction techniques such as mindfulness and relaxation are likely to be helpful. There are many mobile phone apps that you can make use of for this. And focus on diet, exercise, alcohol and tobacco intake limits are all important for teacher health as for everyone else.
2. Think very carefully about work–life balance and how you manage your time. If you say to yourself 'I know I'm working too hard but it's just for now', you need to keep a careful watch on how long 'now' is. Take care that you are not setting up a pattern for your working life that is ultimately unsustainable and doesn't allow for a positive work–life balance. Accept that you can't always do everything and prioritize so that you get the most important activities done. You should include outside work activities with family and friends as an activity in this list. Don't make the mistake of only allocating work tasks high priority in your life for an extended period. Additionally, prioritize which activities are so important that they require focusing all your energies, and which are less important and for which an adequate performance would be sufficient.
3. Build personal and professional networks, both formal and informal. Build these in your school, in your local district, for example learning communities, as well as with the peers that you trained with, and your supervisors or

mentors. Use these networks to get and to give help. This can be questions about classroom management or curriculum instruction, or where personal and professional boundaries are blurring. It is unlikely that the issue you are struggling with is a new one. Don't be afraid to ask.
4. Remind yourself regularly why you decided to become a teacher, what you value in teaching and what is important in what teachers do. You might like to write something down that you can look at from time to time. You want to ensure that you keep in touch with these values, so you are clear about your purpose. There may be times when these feel compromised but staying strong in your commitment to the value of your role in children's future will help you be more resilient at the times when you find the job challenging.
5. Reflect on what went well rather than ruminating on what went wrong. Think of what went wrong as part of a learning process, learn from it ….and move on.
6. Don't strive for perfection in all things. While there are advantages to having ambitious goals and expectations, perfectionism though can have associations with stress and burnout. Don't be too hard on yourself. And in any case, if you are a new teacher it's expected that you won't get everything right all the time.

Annotated bibliography

Eyre, C. (2017). *The elephant in the staffroom: How to reduce stress and improve teacher wellbeing.* **London: Routledge.**
This book is written in easy conversational style and is designed as a practical survival guide for teachers that can be dipped in and out of. It addresses many of the areas that are touched on in this chapter.

Gu, Q. and Day, C. (2007). 'Teachers' resilience: A necessary condition for effectiveness', *Teaching and Teacher Education,* **23, pp. 1302–16.**
This paper reports on a study on resilience in which three resilient teachers were interviewed over four years and illustrates well how they coped with challenges presented at different points in their careers, and the interaction between their professional and personal identities. A good overview of resilience in educators.

Mendonça Mcintyre, T., Mcintyre, S. and Francis, D. (eds.) (2017). *Educator stress: An occupational health perspective.* **New York: Springer International Publishing.**
This edited book brings together an impressive range of international research literature on stress and mental health in the teaching profession from the viewpoint of health and work psychology. It's written for both researchers and practitioners. It provides a rich source for understanding the interrelationship between teaching and stress for someone who wants to explore this area in greater depth.

4
The Social World of the Classroom
Matthew P. Somerville and Ed Baines

Case study

Country: New Zealand/Aotearoa

Year group: Year 5/6 composite classroom (around 9–10 years of age)

Setting: State school situated in a low socio-economic community

Classroom observation (setting up a group activity)

Ms Sua: You're going to work in groups, and I am going to be kind enough to let you choose your groups, but you have to listen first, so you know what to do with your group.

Stella: Oh, Miss?

Ms Sua: Shhhh … listen first.

Ms Sua: With your group you're going to use your map to help you learn about Japan. The first task is to find and locate the places on the map (holds up a blank map and a completed map). So you need to decide where this place is on your map. You need to follow with your eyes the shape of the country and work out with your group where Tokyo will be on your map, and then you need to write what?

Sione: Tokyo!

Ms Sua: Right, put Tokyo on the map. The next question is mark Mt Fuji on the map. Who can tell me where Fuji is on the coloured map?

Stephanie: There (correctly points to Mt Fuji).

Ms Sua: Good. How are we going to get this activity done? What are the things that you need to do with your group to make you successful?

Dave: Work together

Ms Sua: Excellent! What does work together look like?

Sarah: Teamwork

Ms Sua: Right, who can tell us about teamwork?

Sione: It means helping each other, sharing with each other.

Ms Sua: Ok, so basically, you're talking to each other, sharing with each other – so you'll be working together on the same task.

Teacher interview excerpt

In a wide-ranging interview, covering a number of topics, Ms Sua was asked how teachers can best support pupil engagement, learning and well-being. The following was her answer:

Ms: Sua: I don't know, there are too many things I think ... talking with them one-on-one, especially the challenging kids. I notice those who don't want to be here, and I get talking to them and find a moment with them and ask 'What is it that you want to do here in school?' If I ask them once, then they know I'm interested. Then they'll come back the next day and have something to share. I suppose it's gradual, you know how you build relationships with these kids.

Interviewer: So relationships are important to pupil engagement then?

Ms Sua: Yep, I think it has a lot to do with the teachers understanding the kinds of kids you're teaching. What helps for me is that I grew up in a low-income, multicultural school. I think that helps a lot. If you can find something in common with them, you'll get what they need. I mean I come from a family of eight kids, in a state home. I suppose that's why I teach, so they know they don't have to keep that poverty state of mind. This is why I care about their well-being and what they'll be like as adults more than test scores. That's why I teach.

Reflective question

How can you ensure that all pupils within this classroom setup remain engaged?

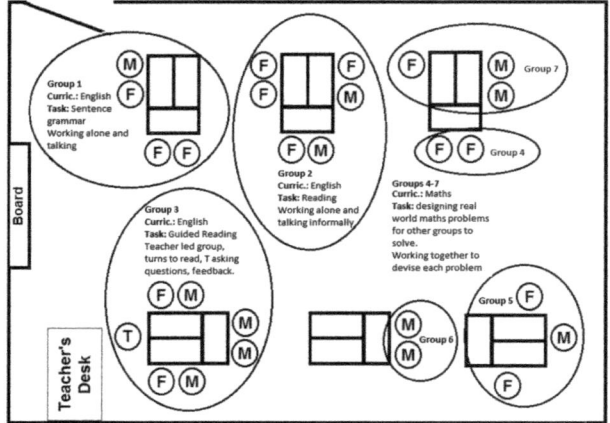

Figure 4.1 Map of Ms Sua's classroom.

Introduction

This case study illustrates the multiple and varied relationships and interactions within which learning takes place. In the classroom observation, you can see an example of whole-class teaching. Ms Sua is presenting to all the pupils in the class, though she still maintains high levels of engagement through her questioning which leads to a number of one-to-one interactions with individual pupils. She is also setting up an activity which requires the pupils to collaborate on a task together in groups.

These interactions highlight how learning is not simply the act of transmitting knowledge from the teacher to the pupil, but rather, a complex series of social interactions which include pupils learning from, and interacting with, one another. Nuthall (2007) argued that pupils simultaneously participate in three different worlds: the public world that teachers see and attempt to manage; the semi-private world of ongoing peer relationships; and the private world of the pupil's own mind. As this chapter is centred around the social context of the classroom, our discussion will be largely focused on the first two of these worlds. Though we do acknowledge the importance of the third – the world in which children's knowledge, beliefs and attitudes continue to change and grow.

In addition to discussing the social context of the classroom, we will be referring to the influence of the physical context of the classroom. Factors such as how the classroom is arranged, the size of the room, seating arrangements, and the number of pupils and adults in the classroom all impact on learning and motivation and need to be considered in any discussion of classroom processes. In Figure 4.1, you can see a map of Ms Sua's classroom. We will be referring to this map throughout the chapter, acknowledging that learning does not take place in isolation, but rather in a distinct physical and social setting.

This chapter provides you with an overview of the literature examining the social context of the classroom and offers practical suggestions on how to create a classroom environment which facilitates close relationships, positive interactions and pupil learning. The chapter begins by examining the nature of the classroom learning environment and how practices such as grouping might influence other processes within the classroom. It considers the importance of teacher–pupil interactions and relationships and interactions among peers – an area that has received relatively little attention when compared to the large body of work focused on teacher interactions. The chapter concludes by looking at the SPRinG project (Baines, Blatchford and Kutnick, 2016) which has used classroom-based research to examine the effectiveness of peer and interactive group work within typical classroom settings.

The nature of the classroom environment

Classroom environments in terms of the available resources, furniture and seating arrangements can differ quite markedly across schools and phases of education as well as between countries. Some schools may have pupils sitting in rows (either of pairs or individuals) facing the front of the classroom. Others may have pupils sitting in groups and yet others may be more flexible, with pupils spending very little time seated in one arrangement. In Figure 4.1, you can see an example of a map of Ms Sua's classroom at one particular point in time. The desks are laid out in a particular way and marked on the map are the pupils indicated by their gender, along with information about the activity that they are undertaking, the location of the teacher and her desk, and the presence of a teaching assistant whom has taken a child outside of the classroom for more intensive and undistracted work.

Consider the different clusters of pupils as 'groupings'. Some are undertaking different activities, some are working on the same task but are somehow separated, others are working fairly independently, while others are supported by an adult. There are additional features of the classroom evident in the map comment such as the number of pupils in the class, the presence of other adults in addition to the teacher and so on. You can gauge from this simple map the complexity of this classroom environment at that particular point in time for teaching and learning and the many factors that Ms Sua would have been thinking about and managing at any one time. At other times, the classroom environment is more straightforward, such as in the classroom observation example when Ms Sua addresses the whole class at once.

There is a trend in educational research to consider the effects of the teacher quite separately from the environment within which teaching and learning take place. But it is important to remember that teachers do not meet individual pupils in isolation but in situ, within a complex classroom environment, where a pupil is surrounded by their peers, doing similar or different things, sometimes as part of a large class, sometimes in a smaller class, with peers of a similar age or with peers of different ages in a mixed-age class. Some schools also organize pupils in classes by ability as you shall see in the following section. These different contextual features have different implications for teaching and learning experiences and the teacher is on the one hand reactive to the classroom environment (e.g. resources available, class size) but also instrumental in setting it up and adapting it for particular purposes (e.g. the seating arrangements or grouping practices for particular activities). The seating arrangement is one way in which the environment may influence learning experiences, with row or horseshoe shape seating far more likely to focus attention to the teacher at the front, while group seating affords the possibility of pupils working together in groups (like in the example map). Some researchers have found that a pupil's seating position within the class can influence their attitude towards learning and their engagement, especially during whole-class activities (see Howe, 2010). There are many aspects of classroom environment that can be considered. We discuss at points in this chapter the influence of class size, and the presence of other adults such as teaching assistants (for more on these factors see Blatchford and Russell, 2020) but next we ask you to think about the use of perceived ability for class organization.

> **Reflective question**
> How can teachers best organize the classroom seating arrangements in a way that allows for different teaching and learning situations?

Ability grouping

One way of organizing the classroom environment beyond considerations of age grouping is in terms of the perceived ability of pupils. Grouping pupils on the basis of an estimate of their academic 'ability' tends to provoke strong views amongst politicians, educators and parents/carers. Some people believe that pupil's attainment can be increased if instruction, learning support, resources, teacher expertise and so on are targeted at groups of pupils that are of a similar level of ability. However, research shows that there are other effects that mean that this ideal cannot be realized and that in fact, grouping by ability has other negative consequences. For example, many have concerns about the potentially divisive effects of grouping pupils by ability and thus prefer mixed-attainment grouping (sometimes referred to as heterogeneous-ability grouping).

One important fact to emphasize in relation to this issue is that accurately establishing a pupil's 'level of ability' is beyond current approaches to testing (see Adey, 2012). Although as a teacher you can capture some estimate of a pupil's attainment in a particular curriculum area, this is only an estimate and does not reflect a pupil's potential or aptitude to learn in that area or indicate a general level of ability. This means that trying to teach at one level will only meet the needs of a few pupils in the class while others struggle to keep up and others are held back.

Ability grouping can take a number of different forms within the school system (see Baines, 2020). Table 4.1 describes the main approaches.

Table 4.1 Forms of ability grouping

Mixed-ability grouping or heterogeneous grouping is where pupils are not organized into classes or groups on the basis of a similar level of ability. They may be organized into groups, but this will reflect the attainment range within the class and school.

Streaming or **tracking** is where pupils are organized into classes for the majority of their lessons on the basis of a general notion of their ability. In these classes, they may receive a particular curriculum that is judged to be of an appropriate level. It can be very difficult for pupils to move class except at transition points (e.g. end of the school year).

Setting or **regrouping** is similar to streaming, but pupils are organized into classes separately for each curriculum area on the basis of ability or attainment in the specific area. Normally the same curriculum is offered and movement between class can be easier than for streaming.

Within-class ability grouping is where pupils within a class are organized into groups on the basis of attainment level, and learning tasks are allocated to those groups based on this level. This form of organization offers the most flexibility when it comes to moving pupils up or down a group and pupils can be in different level groups for different curriculum areas.

Ability grouping' between classes

There has been much research into grouping by ability between classes (most research is on streaming) which shows this approach to be problematic, particularly in relation to equality of opportunity and access to curriculum, resources and instructional expertise. Research has found that when this organization is used, it tends to organize pupils by socio-economic background and across racial lines (Oakes, 2005). Consequently, many argue that it exacerbates and sustains existing societal divisions (Archer et al., 2018).

In terms of attainment, studies show that ability grouping provides little overall benefit for the attainment of all pupils compared to heterogeneous grouping when the curriculum is not differentiated. Where ability grouping is combined with a distinct curriculum for different groups, research shows that high-attaining pupils tend to perform better in similar ability classes, whereas those in the low-ability range tend to fare worse in ability groups than in heterogeneous classes (Hallinan and Kubitschek, 1999; Schoffield, 2010). International research suggests that the earlier ability grouping occurs in childhood, the wider the gap is between the lowest and highest attaining pupils in adolescence (OECD, 2012).

Ability grouping within classes

There has been much less research on the effect of within-class ability grouping. The advantage of within-class grouping over ability grouping between classes is the possibility for a closer relationship with learning and teaching purposes, greater flexibility in movement between groups and greater opportunity for sustained interaction with teachers. Yet even within-class ability grouping can lead to quite varied educational experiences. We know, for instance, that in many primary school classrooms, higher attaining groups tend to receive support and instruction from the teacher, whereas low-attaining groups and pupils with special educational needs are supported by teaching assistants (Baines et al. 2003; Blatchford and Russell, 2020). These persons often have received little to no training in instructional approaches – yet are supporting the pupils that arguably need a greater level of pedagogical expertise. Nevertheless, as within-class ability grouping can be utilized for a range of pedagogic purposes (e.g. group instruction, peer-interactive learning) and may be embedded within a lesson involving other pedagogic practices like whole-class teaching and individual work, they can be used by the teacher in a much more strategic manner (e.g. see Blatchford et al., 2003).

One of the main problems with ability grouping within or between classes is that it can lead to different expectations which become reflected in curriculum demands, through teacher–pupil interaction and teaching practices. These in turn may have marked effects on pupil motivation. Research often conveys a depressing picture of the low-level and fragmented nature of teaching and learning in low-ability groups while more able groups experience more interesting participatory approaches to learning (Dunne et al., 2011; Warrington, 2017; Wiliam and Bartholomew, 2004).

Although there are seemingly obvious advantages to homogenous ability grouping, the evidence is less convincing. Teaching to one level is problematic and without flexible arrangements that enable pupils to change groups, they can become disenchanted with learning. More could be done to make strategic and flexible use of within-class grouping practices for learning purposes. This may mean sometimes strategically mixing abilities for particular activities (e.g. peer learning) and at other times sustaining a more homogenous ability range to enable instruction of small groups. When combined with other instructional approaches, within-class ability grouping may provide motivating, challenging and mutually reinforcing learning contexts that enhance pupil learning while engaging constructively with pupil diversity.

Reflexive questions

1. How were you taught in school?
2. How did it make you feel?
3. Did it have a positive or negative effect on your learning?
4. Thinking about your answers to these questions, do you think your own experiences have influenced the way you like to organize your pupils in class?

> **Reflective question**
> How might you set challenging differentiated activities for all pupils whilst avoiding the pitfalls of fixed ability-based groupings?

Teacher–pupil interactions and relationships

Teacher–pupil relationships

Much of the research on adult–child relations in psychology has focused on relationships between children and parents/carers. This research has been largely informed by Ainsworth and Bowlby's (1991) attachment theory, which defines attachment as an emotional bond that a child forms with another person. The theory posits that secure attachment relationships are more likely to be formed when parents/carers are emotionally available and react to their child in a responsive way. Conversely, the absence of predictable and caring responses to a child's behaviours may lead to an insecure attachment, where the child learns to rely less on their primary caregiver.

More recently, the attachment framework has been extended to the school setting and used to advance the understanding of teacher–pupil relationships. Research evidence indicates that pupils' relationships with teachers matter, particularly for the most vulnerable pupils who may be experiencing less than optimal conditions at home (Pianta, Hamre and Stuhlman, 2003). A high-quality teacher–pupil relationship has been linked with positive functioning across multiple areas, including increased engagement and motivation, higher academic performance, and improved social skills and peer relations (Sabol and Pianta, 2012). The benefits of a positive teacher–pupil relationship also seem to follow positive escalation patterns: high-quality relationships lead to positive experiences, which in turn promote high-quality relationships. These effects seem to be particularly powerful for at-risk pupils, including those with minority status or low maternal education. For these pupils, close teacher–pupil relationships appear to buffer the negative effects associated with disadvantage (Luthar, Cicchetti and Becker, 2000).

Teacher–pupil relationships are typically defined by the attachment-based factors of closeness, conflict and dependency (Pianta, 2001). Closeness refers to having a warm and positive relationship with the pupil – knowing and understanding their needs – something which Ms Sua referred to several times in her interview. Conflict on the other hand refers to the negative aspects of a teacher–pupil relationship.

This factor has been found to be strongly related to subsequent negative outcomes, particularly problematic externalizing behaviours. Finally, dependency describes how possessive or clingy a pupil is with the classroom teacher. High levels of dependency have been linked with acting out behaviours at home and behaviour problems in school (Pianta and Nimetz, 1991). This construct has been considered in research examining the impact of teaching assistants in the classroom. Findings indicate that those pupils who become overly dependent on the teaching assistant limit their contact with both the classroom teacher and their peers (Blatchford et al., 2009).

Classrooms in which teacher–pupil relations appear to be stronger are typically characterized by high levels of pupil autonomy, respect of self and others, a high level of trust and a sense of fairness (Reeve, 2002; Riley, 2004). Teachers demonstrate warmth through positive regard for pupils and pupils feel encouraged, more satisfied with their learning and understand that the teacher is aware of their learning progress (Monsen and Frederickson, 2004). In order to build relations with pupils, teachers also need to recognize and respect what the pupils bring to the classroom – their own background, culture and learning experiences. This was nicely illustrated in the interview with Ms Sua who spoke of how she grew up in a similar neighbourhood to the pupils in her school and how she placed great importance on understanding the pupils' perspectives, struggles and learning needs.

Reflective question
How might pupils' learning and well-being in school be influenced by a positive or a negative relationship with their class teacher?

Teacher expectations

Perhaps the most well-known illustration of teacher expectation effects in the classroom is Rosenthal and Jacobson's (1968) *Pygmalion in the Classroom* study. This involved randomly labelling a small number of pupils as 'bloomers' (likely to progress faster than the other pupils) at the beginning of the school year and comparing their achievement to their classmates at the end of the year. It was found that the bloomers group did in fact progress at a faster rate than their peers, despite there being no real differences in ability between the two groups at the beginning of the year. This difference in progress was attributed to the teachers' higher expectations of the bloomers group.

Although the *Pygmalion in the Classroom* study has been criticized for different methodological reasons over the years, it is still widely accepted that teachers do form expectations about their pupils' skills and abilities and that these expectations are linked to pupils' educational progress. In fact, the focus is less about whether teachers have expectations and more about the accuracy of these expectations.

Why might this be important for you as a teacher?

One of the main concerns regarding teacher expectations is that they may be influenced by certain pupil characteristics such as gender, ethnicity, religion, sexuality or appearance, rather than being purely based on a pupil's academic potential (e.g. Obiakor, 1999; Riegle-Crumb and Humphries, 2012). Additionally, it is possible that these inaccurate expectations could influence teacher–pupil interactions and subsequently pupils' academic progress.

Teacher expectation effects have been categorized into two types: sustaining effects and self-fulfilling prophecies (Rubie-Davies, Hattie and Hamilton, 2010). Sustaining effects describe a situation where the teacher expects pupils to continue to perform at a level based on previously observed patterns and ignore any evidence of changes in pupil performance. In a classroom organized by ability groups, this would make it difficult for a pupil to move from a lower ability group to a higher one. Self-fulfilling prophecy effects are perhaps a more extreme form of teacher expectation effects as they are arguably more likely to lead to changes in pupil behaviour. This is where inaccurate teacher expectations result in pupils performing in a way that is consistent with the initial inaccurate expectations. Thus, if a teacher expects a pupil to perform poorly at school, even if this is based on inaccurate information, there is a tendency for that pupil to perform poorly. These effects may also be in the positive direction with teachers having higher expectations than would be expected based on prior pupil attainment.

Reflexive question
Do you think your own experiences at school have influenced your expectations for some or all pupils you teach now?

Reflective questions
1. What factors influence your expectations for the pupils in your classroom? How confident are you that your expectations are accurate?
2. What can you do to prevent or minimize inaccurate expectations?

What does the research say?

Although the research in this area is complex and at times contradictory, on the whole the evidence suggests that inaccurate teacher expectations do affect teacher actions and ultimately pupils' educational progress (see Blatchford et al., 2016 for a review). However, it appears that inaccurate expectations are only found in approximately one quarter of teachers with the majority of teachers making largely accurate judgements about their pupils (Babad, 2009). Those teachers that do show a bias effect appear to have higher expectations of higher status pupils (e.g., those who are popular with peers) and lower expectations of lower status pupils, such as those who tend to be disruptive in the classroom. The research evidence also indicates that teacher biases are more influential in the early years, highlighting how these early teacher–pupil interactions can continue to influence a pupil's progress throughout their schooling.

How do teacher expectations influence academic progress?

In addition to establishing that there is a link between teacher expectations and pupil's academic progress, it is important to understand why this link exists. The influence of teacher expectations on teacher–pupil interactions is one area that has received a lot of attention. Differences have been found in terms of praise given for good performance, with pupils for whom teachers had high expectations being more frequently praised than pupils for whom they had low expectations. A similar pattern has been found with the amount of work-related interactions, with high-expectation pupils receiving more contact with teachers regarding academic work (Brophy and Good, 1986). This is a somewhat surprising finding given that the lower expectation pupils are arguably more likely to require additional support to complete the work. It has been suggested that this may be due to teachers being more focused on controlling the behaviour of the lower expectation pupils than progressing their learning (Cooper, 1985).

However, in a review of the teacher expectation literature, Blatchford and colleagues (2016) suggest that it is possible that the influence of teacher expectations on teacher–pupil interactions is over-estimated and that the curriculum may play a key role in explaining the link between teacher expectations and pupils' educational progress. If a teacher adjusts the type of work set and level of difficulty of this material based on inaccurate expectations, it is clear to see how this could negatively impact on a pupil's educational progress. Similarly, if organizational practices such as ability grouping or registration for examinations are based on inaccurate teacher beliefs, it could limit a pupil's opportunities – particularly when teacher expectations are considerably lower than a pupil's true academic potential. This effect could be exacerbated in schools in which pupils are placed in classrooms based on teacher estimates of their academic ability at the beginning of the year.

Finally, many of the conceptual models which examine the influence of teacher expectations on pupils' academic progress include a focus on pupil self-perceptions. This relates to the notion of the self-fulfilling prophecy which was discussed earlier. For example, if a teachers' low expectations of a pupil results in fewer academic interactions, an unchallenging curriculum and being placed in a lower ability group, it would not be unreasonable to expect the pupil to notice this differential access to learning and for this to impact on their own expectations of what they can or cannot achieve.

Implications for classroom practice

These findings clearly have implications for your teaching practice. Firstly, the evidence highlights the importance of expecting *all* pupils to progress in their learning. Weinstein (2009) argues that teacher expectations of ability are often too low, too narrow and overly differentiated by factors such as social status. Teacher decisions about curriculum coverage, the types of tasks set and the quality of feedback given should all be based on accurate data with the challenge level set high for all pupils. The research evidence also demonstrates the benefits of viewing pupil abilities as being incremental rather than fixed. As teacher expectations do seem to be passed on to pupils, it seems important for teachers to emphasize effort rather than ability in their interactions with pupils. Incremental views of learning and effort-based beliefs should be reflected in both classroom and school-wide decisions on grouping and differentiating pupils, with all decisions based on pupils' abilities being regularly reviewed.

Reflective questions

1. How can you change your organizational practices and interactions with pupils to reflect an incremental view of learning in your classroom?
2. On entry to school, teachers may assume that summer-born children are a little behind their peers in terms of their learning. How can teachers avoid this perception becoming a self-fulfilling prophecy?

Interactions between teaching staff and pupils

How a teacher or teaching assistant interacts with pupils in class is influenced by a range of factors. Much of the research in this area has focused on teacher characteristics (e.g. training, years of experience) or pupil characteristics (e.g. level of attainment, temperament, motivation). However, contextual factors are likely to be very influential. For example, if you look at Ms Sua's classroom map, you can see that she has her pupils sitting in groups. This allows her to address the whole class, to interact with individual groups, and to interact and support individual pupils. These interactive modes can be broken down further. For example, it is likely her interactions with the two pupils in Group 6 will be different to her interactions with the six pupils in Group 3. These interactions may also vary by the type of task the group is carrying out. For instance, if pupils are engaging in collaborative group work, Ms Sua's interactions may be very minimal, playing more of a supportive role.

In addition to the layout of the classroom, the size of the class is likely to influence adult–pupil interactions. Blatchford and colleagues have written extensively on this topic (e.g. Blatchford et al., 2016), describing in detail how class size is connected with a number of classroom processes, including teacher–pupil interactions. They found that pupils in larger classes were less likely to engage in one-to-one interactions with the teacher, were more likely to experience whole-class teaching and were more likely to engage in passive learning – listening to the teacher, rather than actively initiating and responding to the teacher's talk. Class size also seems to influence group work, with larger classes often having larger groups which can negatively impact on the quality of group work. Although there are studies indicating the effects of class size are not as large as many would expect, it is likely that this is due to teachers not sufficiently adapting their interactions with pupils based on the size of their class, thus not optimizing the benefits of smaller classes (Hattie, 2016).

Another contextual factor to consider is the number of adults in the classroom and how they interact with pupils. Referring back to Ms Sua's map again, you can see there are two adults in this context, though one of them (the teaching assistant) does a lot of their work with individual pupils outside the classroom. This practice clearly reduces the likelihood of teacher–pupil and pupil–pupil interactions for those pupils being removed. This is an example of the teaching assistant providing *alternative* support, rather than support that is *additional* to that provided by the teacher. This is an important distinction to make as research by Radford, Blatchford and Webster (2011) found differences in both the type and quality of interactions between teachers and pupils and teaching assistants and pupils. Teachers were more likely to open up classroom talk, both cognitively and linguistically, and focus on learning and understanding, whereas teaching assistants were found to ask more closed questions and focus on task completion. Researchers from the same team also found a link between these different types of interactions and achievement, with those pupils receiving more teaching assistant support (and therefore less teacher support) performing less well in core subjects, such as English, mathematics and science.

These findings highlight the importance of the language teaching staff use in the classroom. Observation studies of classrooms have found that in many teacher–pupil interactions, the contributions from the pupils tend to be brief and limited. In some instances, this may be due to the types of questions teachers ask in the classroom. An interaction pattern that is common in many classrooms is referred to as the IRF Sequence, which involves the teacher initiating (I) with a question, a pupil responding (R), and the teacher giving feedback based on the pupil's response (F). We can see this in the case study observation data:

Ms Sua: Who can tell me where Fuji is on the coloured map? (**Initiation**)
Stephanie: There (**Response**)
Ms Sua: Good (**Feedback**)

Although this interaction sequence is often seen in almost all classrooms, it has attracted a lot of criticism. It has been described as inauthentic (Cazden, 2001), as it often involves a guessing game in which pupils have to guess what is in the teacher's mind. The sequence typically involves closed questioning, requiring a simple factual answer which is unlikely to assist in developing pupils' learning or understanding. Alexander (2004, p. 24) argues that much of the talk in classrooms does not challenge pupils to think enough and highlights a need for contexts which promote *discussion*, defined as 'the exchange of ideas with a view to sharing information and solving problems' and *dialogue* which aims to achieve 'common understanding through structured questioning and discussion which guides, prompts, and helps in the handover of concepts and principles'. One way of promoting this type of classroom talk is through the use of collaborative group work, an area which will be discussed below.

Reflective question
Reflect on how you challenge your pupils to think. Could you enhance your practice? How and when?

Peer relations and interactions

When thinking about classroom contexts, you will most often think of them in terms of the adults and their interactions and relationships with pupils. It would not be surprising if you view the teacher as the expert, the person who knows what needs to be taught and who needs to impart this knowledge somehow to the pupils in the class. We can easily overlook the important influence other pupils in the class can have on their peers. A child's peers are usually only considered in terms of their potential disruptive effect. For example, teachers are often concerned about the role of peers in off-task chatter, behavioural disruption between pupils and about peers copying each other's work (Epstein, 1983). Yet it is important to recognize that pupils spend the majority of their time in the company of their peers, and, given their number, are far more likely to interact with them than with adults. Children have their own ideas about the nature of the world, and they are often keen to share these ideas through their interactions with each other (informally or more formally arranged). It is important to acknowledge that peers can influence classroom life in positive ways. They can be an important resource for enhancing and supporting learning in the class, for facilitating inclusion, and for making learning enjoyable (and thus school becomes more meaningful and engaging). In fact, as you shall see, learning in some situations can be more powerful when it involves peers than when it is directed by an adult.

There are some fundamental ways in which you can think about the relations between peers. Some pupils are popular with their classmates while others may be less accepted or even rejected by them. Within the class there will also be pupils who are friends, possibly best friends or just play companions, while others may never get along, and some may bully others or be the victims of bullying. The teacher needs to understand these relationships, their changing nature over time and the possible implications for interaction, learning and behaviour in the classroom. For example, the teacher may need to think carefully about where to seat a pupil who is often bullied by peers. Seating pupils that are good friends together can have positive consequences for learning, but in other circumstances may have negative consequences.

One important research finding in terms of peer relations in classrooms is that those pupils who are more accepted or popular are more likely to do well in school. Such pupils tend to be more prosocial, are more able to regulate their behaviour and have a better awareness of other people's perspectives. On the other hand, pupils who have difficulties with peers and who are less accepted or possibly rejected by peers are likely to do less well academically (Blatchford et al., 2016).

The explanations for these associations between acceptance by peers and academic attainment effects are not obvious, but there are a range of possible reasons. For instance, it may be that those pupils that are better adjusted both socially and academically are more liked. Alternatively, it may be that pupils that are well liked tend to be more cooperative or prosocial and thus receive and give more help and engage in positive learning supportive interactions within class. There may also be a sense in which those pupils that are rejected are more likely to feel distressed, depressed and lonely which may not put them in a good state of mind for learning. They may also be keen to 'play up' to peers, possibly by being disruptive or by becoming a 'class clown', in order to ingratiate themselves with peers.

When it comes to the issue of friends, teachers often suggest that they would not normally allow friends to sit or work together (Baines et al., 2003). This is because of the view that friends will be more likely to draw each other off task. However, research studies suggest that this may depend on the context and nature of the activity. In a review of this literature, Zajac and Hartup (1997) found that when the task set is fairly easy, mundane or repetitive then friends may function to distract each other. On the other hand, when tasks are challenging and involve the solving of problems, friendship pairs are far more likely to outperform pairs of pupils who are not friends. This difference is explained by friends being better at cooperating together and being more thoughtfully engaged. During challenging tasks, talk between friends tends to involve more elaboration and checking of progress and when disputes arise, they tend to be resolved through reasoning talk rather than squabbling. This is maybe not surprising since friends are more committed and secure in each other's company. They are more likely to speak up and to help each other. Other research suggests that the trend for friends working well together may be far more likely amongst girls, and more able girls in particular, than boys (Kutnick and Kington, 2005).

Just as peers can influence what happens in the classroom, the physical organization of the classroom and the ethos and the approach to teaching adopted by the teacher can influence the nature of pupils' relationships with each other. A number of studies highlight that proximity and similarity is what draws children together to form friendships. The upshot of this is that seating and grouping in class can influence the formation of friendships. If the classroom is arranged by attainment, by gender, or inadvertently by ethnicity or socio-economic status, this can have important implications for pupils' socialization. Teachers can also have an important effect on how certain pupils are perceived. For example, studies have shown that teacher praise and behaviour towards different pupils in the class can influence the way they are perceived by their peers (Flanders and Havumaki, 1960). In classes where teachers praise prosocial and helpful behaviour and encourage a sense of community involving attention to social and moral development, peer groups are more supportive and pupils perceive a higher level of emotional support (Wentzel, 2009). There is, therefore, an important way in which teacher–pupil relations, peer relations and academic outcomes may be connected.

Cooperative and collaborative group work

The informal interactions and relationships between peers become all the more important during times when the teacher asks pupils to work together either with a partner or in small groups to undertake a task. This is an important approach in any teacher's tool kit and is particularly useful for pupil's learning. This is an example of what some refer to as 'peer co-learning' and there are a range of different types including 'peer tutoring', where one child with greater expertise in the topic helps a less knowledgeable child to do something; 'cooperative learning', which relates to situations when pupils in pairs or small groups help and support each other to learn and understand new material; and 'collaborative learning', where pupils work together to achieve a joint goal. This might involve shared thinking and reasoning, to solve a problem, make a decision or plan an activity.

These different approaches stem from the theoretical ideas of Vygotsky and Piaget, two key child developmental theorists in the twentieth century (see Howe, 2010). There is much research that has highlighted the huge potential of peer co-learning approaches, for pupils' attainment and learning, positive motivational and social attitudes, and for positive peer relationships (Johnson and Johnson, 2013; Slavin et al., 2014). These approaches are of particular value when pupils undertake tasks involving the application and consolidation of their knowledge and skills (Kutnick and Blatchford, 2014).

The possible reasons why peer co-learning approaches may support deeper learning are because they encourage participants to articulate and explain their thinking, listen to the thinking of others and to build on each other's new ideas. During this process, group members must also (re-)structure and clarify their ideas, which consolidates their understanding, their awareness of what they know and what they do not know, and discrepancies between their own understanding and that of others. Sometimes the need to resolve conflicts during collaborative learning situations arises and this prompts pupils to provide complex explanations, counter arguments and counter evidence (Baines et al., 2009; Doise and Mugny, 1984; see Howe, 2010). Collaborative learning has been found to encourage pupils to take responsibility for their own learning rather than being passive recipients of knowledge.

Recent debates about the purpose of education and the nature of the skills that pupils should gain from their school experiences often highlight the importance of so-called twenty-first-century skills. This is an umbrella term for a range of skills, behaviours and characteristics, including the ability to solve problems, communicate effectively and to work as part of a team. These skills are essential for current and future work environments (Luckin et al., 2017). Nevertheless, despite the positive evidence and an apparent need within society, studies of everyday classroom practices show that pupils are often found seated in groups but rarely are asked to work together in a meaningful or purposeful way (Baines et al., 2003; Galton et al., 1999). Nor is it the case that schools provide opportunities for pupils to develop the skills that underpin group working. These skills are often taken for granted and assumed to develop naturally through everyday interactions with others. While some may naturally develop skills involved in working as part of a team, many others will only learn them in part.

Other research indicates that sometimes teachers and pupils have concerns about the value of working together. Teachers, in particular, can have concerns that group work can lead to reduced classroom control, reduced pupil engagement and the increased possibility of poor behaviour (Gillies and Boyle, 2010). Pupils, on the other hand, are unsure about group work because they are often told to avoid sharing information or copying and because working with others can be difficult and sometimes frustrating (Galton and Williamson, 1992).

Reflective questions

1. Do you have any concerns about group work in your own classroom?
2. What has/hasn't worked for you in the past?

So how can you, as a teacher, overcome these concerns and make best use of peer co-learning methods? Adopting peer co-learning is not as simple as placing pupils in groups and then asking them to work together to undertake a learning task. A few key features need to be in place in order for working together to be successful. According to researchers (Johnson and Johnson, 2013), there are at least three main areas that need to be addressed for peer co-learning to be successful. These essential features are:

1. Group members must be positively interdependent (i.e. the activity cannot be successfully completed by one person alone, but all group members must recognize that they all need to synchronize their efforts);
2. Group members must engage in promotive interaction and show a willingness to support each other in their joint efforts to complete the activity and achieve the goal (e.g. helping each other, challenging each other's reasoning, explaining their own ideas and suggestions, providing feedback, as well as supporting the inclusion of other members);
3. Group members must be individually accountable – they must make sure that they undertake their share of the work and also ensure that others undertake theirs. This means that all group members feel personally responsible for the group's success in completing the task. Individual accountability can be promoted within groups by ensuring the activity is designed to enhance positive interdependence or by ensuring that individual contributions to group effort are transparent.

Other researchers suggest that when introducing peer co-learning to school-aged children, it needs to be accompanied by efforts to develop the interpersonal and group skills that underpin peer co-learning along with opportunities for group reflection (Kutnick and Blatchford, 2014). Some programmes harness group reflection to enhance the explicit learning and application of group working skills (see the SPRinG project in the Window on research).

Researchers have studied how to improve peer co-learning. It is useful to consider the physical and social context of the group, the skills and relationships of group members, the structure and nature of the activity that group members must engage with, and the role of adults or teachers in supporting and assisting the groups in their purpose (Baines et al., 2016). A consideration of the context of the group interaction is also important, for example, in terms of the size and composition of the group, and the physical positioning of members so that they can easily see and hear each other. Pupils can find the task of communicating in a group cognitively challenging which means that they find it easier to manage complex tasks in pairs or smaller groupings (Baines and Howe, 2010).

The importance of positive relationships within the group for successful working together calls for members to develop an understanding of each other, through activities designed to develop sensitivity and trust. Johnson and Johnson (2013) highlight the importance of these social qualities for effective group relationships but note that these are dynamic qualities that are continuously changing over time. An individual may be skilled at understanding others but whether they show sensitivity and trust will depend on the developing relationship between members of the group. Repeated experiences of working together allow group understanding and commitment to develop.

Research by Webb and colleagues (2017) has emphasized that effective group work relies on sophisticated communication between group members and emphasizes the importance of the provision of explanations and help seeking and giving behaviours. Similarly, others have emphasized the importance of collaborative discussion or exploratory talk between group members. Such talk involves the exploration and provision of different lines of discussion, explanations, counter arguments, clarificatory questions and the exploration of different potential solutions to problems (Baines and Howe, 2010; Mercer et al., 2017). Effective groups need to be able to utilize effective communication strategies, but also must be able to manage and resolve points of conflict in positive ways.

Other research has focused on the aspects of the activity that pupils engage with when working together and how these can be best set up to enable good-quality working together and effective learning (Howe and Tolmie, 2003). This is an important component for you as a teacher to get right and is not easily achieved in the general absence of ready-made materials or lesson plans for teachers wanting to undertake peer co-learning. More recently, researchers have examined the key role of teachers and adults in supporting, structuring and facilitating positive peer co-learning experiences (Webb et al., 2017) as well as in assisting pupils to develop the necessary skills that underpin successful working together with peers.

In order to use peer co-learning methods, teachers require a high level of training so that they can organize their classes and learning tasks to be undertaken in ways that ensure the work is effective. Unfortunately, training in peer co-learning approaches is often not covered well in teacher training programmes. There are, however, a range of different programmes and approaches designed to support teachers in developing peer co-learning approaches in primary school settings. One such programme arose out of the SPRinG project, undertaken by Blatchford et al. (2005), which aimed to develop a new and straightforward approach to peer co-learning, grounded in the practicalities and reality of everyday classroom settings and the concerns of teachers and pupils.

Reflexive questions

1. How did you feel about co-learning as a pupil?
2. Have these past experiences influenced your teaching practice?

Reflective question

What could you do to optimize peer co-learning in your classroom?

Window on research

How to improve the effectiveness of group work in schools: The SPRinG project

Baines, E., Blatchford, P. and Kutnick, P. (2017). *Promoting effective group work in the primary classroom: A handbook for teachers and practitioners*. 2nd edn. London, UK: Routledge

The SPRinG (Social Pedagogic Research into Groupwork) research project was part of the Teaching and Learning Research Programme, a national programme of UK research. The project had two aims: first, to work with primary and secondary school teachers to develop strategies which would enhance the quality of group and paired work; and, second, to evaluate whether these strategies would result in an improvement in pupils' attainment and learning, behaviour and attitudes to learning.

The SPRinG project was undertaken over a 5-year period. Initially the researchers worked with teachers to develop the programme that could be easily integrated into school life and the curriculum, and that recognized the practical concerns and difficulties teachers can have with group work. The approach was also informed by theory and research evidence and was trialled in primary and secondary schools.

The resulting programme handbook provides teachers with a set of recommended strategic practices for setting up their classroom and groups for group work, for developing group work activities, for understanding how best to support and facilitate group working, and most importantly, for developing the necessary skills amongst pupils to support effective group working.

The programme was evaluated by comparing the effects of the programme on pupils involved in SPRinG with those in classes that were part of a control group (that did not undertake SPRinG group work), over the course of a year. The evaluation examined effects on pupils' academic progress, their behaviour, interaction and talk in the classroom during the school day and in terms of their attitudes towards working together. Teachers were also interviewed about their experiences and views.

Findings showed:

- Far from impeding learning, there was evidence that showed that group work raised levels of attainment and deeper conceptual understanding and inferential thinking. This was the case for all pupils.
- Despite some teachers' worries that group work might be disruptive, pupil behaviour improved in the SPRinG classes. Pupils were able to take more responsibility for their own behaviour and learning, freeing up teacher time to observe and reflect upon classroom activities.
- Group work doubled pupils' levels of sustained, active engagement in learning and more than doubled the amount of high-level, thoughtful discussion between pupils.

The study also found that teachers valued the SPRinG approach to group work and felt that it developed their skills and confidence and, in some cases, were released from a focus on controlling activities to more time spent on teaching.

What is unique about SPRinG?

There are different approaches to enhancing collaborative group work. SPRinG aims to help pupils develop the skills in a supportive situation and during tasks that are conducive to working together. SPRinG aims to provide teachers with simple and practical strategies for facilitating group working that complement other approaches to teaching and learning and that can form part of a strategic approach to classroom teaching and learning.

Simple strategies include ensuring that younger pupils work in pairs for more complex tasks and that older pupils do not work in groups of any more than four until they are experienced at working with others. Seating pupils around a single table or at the corners of tables enables pupils to get closer together, to see each other, and reduces the noise levels that can so often put teachers off using peer co-learning approaches.

What do we learn?

The SPRinG study raises all sorts of implications for classroom practice when it comes to Collaborative Group Work. At the heart of the programme is the idea that pupils need to have some training in social, communication and group problem-solving skills and in order to support this, teachers need to help pupils to reflect on their developing skills. It is also important for teachers to consider how they can connect collaborative group work in a strategic way with other forms of teaching and learning and to think carefully about what effective collaborative group work may look like and sound like.

More information on SPRinG available at http://www.spring-project.org.uk

Reflective questions

1. How do we know when groups of pupils are working well together?
2. What does effective collaborative group work look like and sound like?
3. How can teachers support pupils to reflect on and improve their own skills in working together with others?

Conclusion

This chapter has examined the social world of the classroom. It has used a case study to highlight a range of social contextual factors related to pupil's learning, including the nature of the classroom environment, ability grouping, teacher–pupil relationships, teacher expectations, interactions between teaching staff and pupils, peer relations and interactions, and cooperative and collaborative group work. We have conveyed the complexity of these interactions and relationships within the classroom and have highlighted the fact that much of the educational literature considers the effects of the teacher quite separately from the environment within which teaching and learning take place. We argue that learning does not take place in isolation, but rather in a distinct physical and social setting that, in itself, can influence the teaching and learning process. Subsequently, any discussion or decisions made about pupil learning must consider the processes and social contextual factors presented in this chapter.

Annotated bibliography

Blatchford, P., Pellegrini, A. and Baines, E. (2016). *The child at school: Interactions with peers and teachers.* **2nd edn. London, UK: Routledge**
This book examines how relationships and interactions with peers, teachers and other school staff influence children's development and how they experience school. It includes many of the topics we have touched on in this chapter and extends the discussion to other contexts such as the playground. The content will be of interest and relevance to both trainee and practising teachers.

Howe, C. (2010). *Peer groups and children's development.* **Oxford: Wiley Blackwell**
The focus of this text is on peer groups in primary and secondary school pupils. It considers both classroom and out-of-class settings and how interactions within these settings relate to pupils' personal, intellectual and social development. It includes a number of topics that are likely to be of direct relevance to trainee and practising teachers, such as the structure of classroom subgroups, whole-class and subgroup interaction, and the influence of peer status and friendships in the classroom.

Nuthall, G. (2007). *The hidden lives of learners.* **Wellington, New Zealand: NZCER Press**
This book explores the three worlds which shape a pupil's learning: the public world that teachers see and attempt to manage; the semi-private world of ongoing peer relationships; and the private world of the pupil's own mind. It draws upon Nuthall's meticulous recordings of classroom conversations over a period of forty years. It was written with classroom teachers and teacher educators in mind and is an excellent resource for helping us understand how pupils learn through their interactions with other pupils and teaching staff.

Pollard, A., Black-Hawkins, K., Cliff-Hodges, G., Dudley, P., Higgins, S., James, M., Linklater, H., Swaffield, S., Swann, M., Winterbottom, M. and Wolpert, M.A. (2019). *Reflective teaching in Schools.* **5th edn. London, UK: Bloomsbury Publishing.**
This book has been written for both students and professionals, from those in initial teacher training to expert teachers. Part 2, in particular, focuses on the content areas we have discussed in the current chapter. It considers learning environments – both formal and informal – and how these are shaped by interactions and relationships. Other areas such as inclusion, engagement and managing behaviour are examined, drawing upon a combination of practitioner experience and contemporary research. As the title suggests, throughout the book, the reader is encouraged to consider how they can better understand pupil development and enhance the quality of their own teaching.

5
Effective Interpersonal Communication

Jeremy Monsen, Linda Crichton and Julie Shaw

Whatever competence means today, we can be sure its meaning will have changed by tomorrow. The foundation for future professional competence seems to be the capacity to **learn how to learn** *(Schein, 1972 – emphasis added). This requires developing one's own continuing theory of practice under real-time conditions.*

(Argyris and Schön, 1974, p. 157)

Introduction

As teachers we need to be able to communicate effectively and jointly problem solve with a wide range of people, sometimes under challenging circumstances. This is a core skill that needs to be mastered by all teachers. For the vast majority of communications that you have at school there will be no issues or misunderstandings.

Yet, there may be times when it becomes very apparent that an encounter or interaction is proving to be difficult and not going as you had planned. Paradoxically, it is through these communications that you have an opportunity to learn how to do things differently, and potentially more successfully, if, you are open to exploring your own behaviour and what may be underpinning it.

Often, indications that something is not going as well as planned include a sense of annoyance, unease, discomfort, confusion or that sensation that the hairs on the back of your neck are rising! Experience or intuition alone is not sufficient to enable you to engage in this reflective task and identify the factors causing the difficulties. You need a framework that can support you to clarify what beliefs and values underpin your actions (in this case verbal behaviours, referred to in this chapter as Guiding Principles and by Argyris and Schön, 1974, as Governing Variables), to test out new ways of acting, and to take on greater personal responsibility.

The case study shared in the next section clearly did not go as planned for Michelle; a newly qualified teacher (NQT), who was left feeling frustrated and probably rather demoralized following her discussion with Mandy (a Learning Support Assistant, LSA). Michelle had hoped to facilitate a 'frank and honest' discussion with Mandy about some of the issues she had, from her perspective. Michelle had unilaterally assumed that Mandy shared her own world view, and would therefore naturally confirm her understanding, when directly asked the questions 'what was going well?' and also 'what was not going so well?'.

Case study: A difficult conversation between a beginning teacher and their link LSA

Country: England, UK

Age group: Primary/Elementary school level, a class of 7-year-olds

Setting: Mainstream state-funded school

Participants involved: A beginning teacher Michelle Ammar and her LSA Mandy Bryant.

The case study:

Background and context

This case study involves a meeting between an NQT (Michelle Ammar) and a LSA (Mandy Bryant).

Michelle is a 25-year-old graduate with a first-class honours degree in education. She undertook a 1-year postgraduate training course to obtain her teaching qualifications. She is used to being seen as competent and successful, receiving 'outstanding' grades for her teaching practices as a student teacher. She started her first teaching job at St Mary's primary/elementary school, which is located in a socio-economically mixed community within a large inner city approximately one term ago. Although completing her initial teacher education very successfully, like many NQTs Michelle is finding the reality of having a class of her own both stimulating and challenging in various respects.

Mandy Bryant is a 50-year-old woman who works as a LSA at St Mary's. In her previous career, Mandy worked as a marketing executive in the business sector, but wanting to spend more time with her family, she decided 10 years previously to undertake part-time work near her home and children's schools. Mandy believes that she has a wealth of personal and professional transferable skills and experience from her former business career which she brings to her job at the school. Mandy's eldest daughter happens to be Michelle's age.

A meeting was called near the end of Michelle's first term due to her concerns that Mandy was dominating and taking over within the classroom and not following directions as Michelle, the class teacher had expected. Michelle is concerned that Mandy's main focus is on getting the set work for the lesson completed and for there to be plenty of work evidenced in books, at the expense of quality of learning and secure understanding and achievement of the lesson intention by the children. Sometimes, Michelle felt that Mandy was overly 'helping' children arrive at answers, in order to rush through the work. Michelle felt that the children were receiving some 'mixed' messages about what was expected of them (lots of work in books from Mandy, less but higher quality work and discussion with children from Michelle) resulting in the general progress of the children in lessons being below expectations. This was causing Michelle a great deal of stress, frustration and sleepless nights, as she would soon be coming up for a review of her progress where children's attainment would be under scrutiny. Her NQT supervisor Anna Connaught suggested that Michelle try and talk with Mandy to resolve things, so they could both start the new term afresh, with a clearer understanding of what was to be achieved in the classroom, what specifically Mandy should be helping the children with and where her focus should be. The key aim was for them to be able to work more effectively and with greater impact together. If this did not work then Anna suggested that a more formal, three-way meeting might be necessary.

Michelle's implicit purpose was to give Mandy honest feedback, to clarify expectations, and to obtain a clear commitment from her that she understood what the issues were, and that she would try to focus more clearly on the understanding of the children so that things would be different in the new term. Michelle's intention was that with Mandy working more in the manner that Michelle envisaged, Mandy would therefore have more impact on the children's learning and progress. The proposed meeting had come as a surprise to Mandy as she had not been given a clear and specific reason for the meeting. However, in her experience, she had seen many NQTs struggle with managing the demands of the job particularly, in the early months and has been aware that, at times, Michelle has appeared frustrated. Mandy's perspective was that Michelle was exhibiting her inexperience and required help to fully meet the learning needs of the children and complete the work set within the lesson. Mandy, from her perspective, was doing her best to ensure the work was completed, and that all children she worked with in the class had plenty of work recorded in their books. After all, as a valued member of staff, with 10 years of experience and four children of her own, Mandy believed she was well equipped to do this and was used to working with that year group and with NQTs.

This is a segment of their interaction:

Michelle – 'Thanks very much for agreeing to meet me. I know it's the end of the day and we have both had an exhausting time, especially this afternoon'. 'Would you like a cup of tea?' [Trying to be relatable and positive].

Mandy – 'Yes that would be good but, I can make it. What would you like?' [Unsure as to why they are meeting].

[A few minutes later, with tea made]

Michelle – 'Well, the reason I wanted to meet was to check with you how you think things are going in the classroom? As you know, I only started in September and it's been a really busy term with a lot to get established.' [Wanting to be clear and authoritative, in charge and in control. Michelle would like Mandy to share her perspective and agree with her but, has not provided any concrete examples.]

Mandy – 'Yes it has. I've worked with a lot of teachers, many of them NQTs, in my time at the school, and I've seen how it can take a while to establish routines and get the children settled … ' [Mandy is thinking, I'm not sure what she's getting at or what she expects me to say, what is this meeting really about?].

Michelle – 'Oh … I am … I meant, you know, if we are going to work together really effectively and with the new term not far away … I was just wondering, you know, whether you had any feedback for me on what you think is going well, and what's not going so well, especially about how well the children are learning, how much progress they're making, that sort of thing really ….' [Beginning to feel uncomfortable and unsure what to say as she does not want to hurt Mandy's feelings or cause offence by seeming to be accusatory or too direct so does not share her real concerns and hopes that Mandy will discern these from what she seems to be implying].

Mandy – 'Well, I can't think of anything in particular that isn't working, as I said, I've worked with many NQTs and I know my job very well. As you probably know, I'm very experienced, and I'm good at getting all of the children to finish their work and get lots in their books … do you think there is a problem?' [Still unclear as to the real point of the meeting, but, beginning to get the feeling that it may have something to do with her].

Michelle – 'Oh no … not a problem, as you know I try to be very organised and I think I've got all the lesson planning up to date for the rest of this term. I was just wondering what more you could do to maybe, help me out, to make sure that the children clearly understand what they need to do with their table tasks and small group work, and what the learning is behind it. You know, so that they not only complete the tasks that are set, according to the lesson plans, but that they understand the concepts, and point of the learning, so that the lesson intention, is always met.' [Michelle is really feeling uncomfortable because Mandy has not raised or appears to recognize the issues she wants to discuss and resolve, and doesn't seem to be aware at all of the issues as Michelle sees them].

Mandy – 'Well, I know what I have to do, get the resources ready for the lesson and I work with the groups, explaining to them, showing them if they seem unsure about what they need to do so they always complete their work, and when you're not here, I sometimes cover the class. But as I said, I'm very experienced and I don't mind doing this. Do you feel I'm not doing something right?' [Beginning to feel some implied criticism and becoming increasingly defensive and annoyed as Michelle doesn't be able to explain herself or the issues in a way that she properly understands].

Outcome

The meeting ends with Michelle feeling that she has not fulfilled her goal of addressing the issues she feels exist, giving Mandy clear feedback and securing her understanding and willingness to make what Michelle feels are necessary changes. This, she feels, is because Mandy is naturally over-confident, and potentially, a difficult person to challenge. Michelle feels the age difference may be a factor, and that Mandy does not necessarily respect Michelle as being the leader in the classroom, thinking that 'she (Mandy) could do a better job'. Michelle wonders whether Mandy possibly resents her for being so well-qualified (although, Mandy has a degree in marketing, had a senior post and was successful in her earlier career which is unknown to Michelle). The meeting ends on a rather uncomfortable note. Michelle worries that the discussion has not helped and their relationship may deteriorate next term. This thought causes her further distress. Mandy, on the other hand, has been left bemused, confused and a little annoyed, as she is still unclear as to the real purpose of the meeting and what exactly the problems were that Michelle was trying to communicate. This reinforces for Mandy her belief that Michelle is indeed inexperienced, particularly in terms of communicating in a professional manner, and really does need her support and the benefit of her substantial experience. However, Mandy is now wary, feeling indirectly criticized. It is highly likely that both people will carry on as before possibly, slightly less cooperatively if the misunderstanding is not addressed adequately and communication improved.

Reflective questions

1. Does this interaction trigger any memories of similar encounters you may have had?
2. How did you react at the time and how did you manage the situation?
3. Did you feel satisfied with the outcomes?
4. Did you want to do things differently but, did not know what to do?

It is hoped that the **Accessible Dialogue** framework, based as it is upon the work of Argyris and Schön (1974, 1996, who used the terms Model II or 'Critical Dialogue') and Robinson (2018, who developed the model into 'Learning Conversations' to inform whole school improvement), and further developed for use with trainee educational and child psychologists and teachers by Cameron and Monsen (1998), may help you avoid such difficult and negative, or unproductive conversations, as outlined in the case study.

Within the English context the term 'Critical' had negative connotations and so the term 'Accessible' was chosen instead, in order to emphasis the idea of making one's thinking accessible to others, open and collaborative with the aim of engendering more satisfying and productive relationships and outcomes.

Once understood and practised, it can be used to clarify what may underpin your current communications style and provide a basis for testing out new ways of acting so different and more effective outcomes can occur.

This chapter provides you with an outline of the theoretical basis underpinning the approach, its key components (framed in operational terms so they are easy to execute and practise) and guidance regarding how to apply, gain feedback, reflect and develop skills over the course of your teaching career.

The importance of developing effective communication skills within teaching practice

One of the key tasks that teachers need to perfect during the course of their careers is the ability to effectively communicate and jointly problem solve during those times when some interactions with colleagues, other practitioners, parents/carers and pupils are challenging.

There is little evidence to suggest that teachers' communication and problem-solving skills improve with experience and practice alone (Lichtenberg, 1997). For sustained development to occur at least three requirements must be in place:

1. Accurate feedback regarding the interaction from the perspectives of both parties based upon what actually occurred, rather than what was assumed to have occurred (this is the match or mismatch between what you had planned to say and do, what actually happened and how it was perceived by the other person).
2. The use of a framework (like Accessible Dialogue) to help structure and guide the process of clarifying, testing and accepting personal responsibility for the consequences of our actions, both, intended and unintended.

3. The motivation to want to reduce the gap between what you said you would do and what actually occurred.

Unless these factors are in place, there will be an increased likelihood of personal bias and self-fulfilling beliefs relating either to yourself (tending to be more positively skewed) or to others (tending to be more negatively skewed) (Blatchford, Pellegrini and Baines, 2016).

Croll and Moses (1985) found that primary/elementary teachers when asked to offer explanations for some of the behaviour issues of pupils in their classes referred to within-child or home-based factors in over 80 per cent of cases.

The teachers had little power to act upon or alter significantly these within-child or home-based factors. Yet, by contrast, school- or teacher-related factors, such as curriculum and classroom behaviour management, level of differentiation, questioning and feedback and interpersonal style, were referred to in less than 4 per cent of cases. These factors as opposed to within-child and home-based aspects are much more amenable to analysis and change. The teachers sampled did not identify these in their reasoning about what could be contributing to the problems within their classes.

Similarly, evidence of bias exists within interpersonal communications and problem-solving. Argyris and Schön (1974, 1996) argue that there are universal, human characteristics which underpin the design of our actions (in our case verbal behaviour). These characteristics that give consistency and coherence to our actions from one time to the next are intuitive and conform to the following core beliefs and values or Guiding Principles:

- To unilaterally pursue my own agendas and goals;
- To maximize my 'winning' and minimize my 'losing';
- To minimize eliciting negative feelings in the other person;
- To be rational and minimize emotionality;
- To believe that publically testing my assumptions or attributions is a risky strategy best to be avoided.

These tacit Guiding Principles encourage people like Michelle, to look at others (Mandy) and the environment, and not themselves when reflecting upon the reasons as to why things do not go so well. The purpose of such beliefs and values is to avoid embarrassment or personal threat, challenge or, feelings of vulnerability or incompetence. Paradoxically, they may well contribute to these very feelings. These are referred to as Model I Communication Strategies by Argyris et al. (1974, 1996 see Table 5.1).

An alternative set of Guiding Principles aimed at achieving a different set of more constructive outcomes during communications and problem-solving are referred to as Model II or Critical Dialogue by Argyris et al. (1974, 1996) (see Table 5.2) and this forms the basis of the Accessible Dialogue approach described in this chapter.

Table 5.1 Model I – Strategies aimed at controlling and winning

1 Guiding principles	2 Interpersonal environment created	3 Communication strategies employed	4 Illustrations	5 Consequences for participants and their learning
Pursue own agendas, purposes and goals	Develop an interpersonal environment in which one participant controls the factors that are relevant to them.	**Advocacy** (you only partially disclose information, which is framed in a way which is difficult to test out and which pushes your views and positions) • **Minus illustration** (you do not provide many examples of what you actually mean) • **Minus reasoning** (you do not provide the reasoning behind your views) • **Minus inquiry** (you do not check out your views or thinking with others)	**Don't say what you think** (when you think it might upset others and when you privately judge that saying it is not to your own advantage or gain)	• It is likely that participants will be perceived as being defensive. • It is likely that at least one participant will perceive 'hidden agendas' operating and a lack of openness and trust.
Maximize 'winning' and minimize 'losing'	One participant manages the interaction/dialogue and its tasks for their own hidden purposes.	**Inferences** (you infer certain attributes and/or evaluate others and events) • **Minus illustration** (you do not provide specific examples of what led you to a particular attribute or evaluation) • **Minus inquiry** (you do not check out the adequacy of your views or thinking with others)	**Don't say why you think it** (because the correctness of your views is obvious, you expect compliance and you are confident of their worth)	• It is likely that interpersonal relationships and group dynamics will be perceived as being defensive. • It is likely that there will be limited public testing of theories and inferences.

Minimize eliciting negative feelings	Protection of self is a unilateral task and oriented towards control and achievement of their goals.	***Inquiry*** (you ask questions or make comments to control and manipulate the discussion. This is often disguised as you ***advocating for valid information***)	
		Don't check out your understanding with others (when trying to persuade them, or when expecting others to think as you do since your views are obvious and right)	• It is likely that non-learning-oriented norms will develop. • It is likely that problem-solving effectiveness will be decreased because of limited access to and quality of the information produced. • It is likely that single-loop learning processes will develop.
Be rational and minimize emotionality	The protection of others, including difficult or emotional charged issues is a unilateral task.	***Don't embed dialogue within an interpersonal style***, which encourages openness, but instead results in non-disclosure of valid information, avoids emotional issues and involves the unilateral control of the process.	• It is likely that participants will perceive low freedom of choice, internal commitment to ideas and change and decreased risk taking. • It is likely that emotional issues, which are ignored, will jeopardise problem-solving effectiveness in the future ('revenge cycles').

Table 5.2 Accessible Dialogue – Strategies aimed at guiding more effective interpersonal problem-solving

1 Guiding principles	2 Interpersonal environment created	3 Communication strategies employed	4 Illustrations	5 Consequences for participants and their learning
To increase valid information for all participants so that problem-solving effectiveness is improved.	Develop an interpersonal environment in which participants can experience a high degree of personal autonomy and causation.	**Advocacy** (you make your views, the reasoning behind them and their fallibility explicit to the other person[s]) • **Plus illustration** (you share specific evidenced examples of what you mean) • **Plus reasoning** (you share your 'theory' about these events in a way which enables them to be tested out) • **Plus inquiry** (you check out with others the adequacy of your views and 'theories')	**You say what you think** (within the terms of your professional relationship, rather than hide what you think and operate as if it was self evident and correct) 'Sally when I observed you yesterday doing the INSET on Literacy I was wondering why you didn't include reference to Clay's material.'	• It is likely that participants will be perceived as being minimally defensive. • It is likely that participants will perceive that any 'hidden agendas' are open to debate and discussion. • It is likely that participants will perceive higher degrees of openness and trust.
To enhance free and informed choice to any agreement or understanding reached	The dialogue and its tasks are jointly managed.	**Inferences** (you infer certain attributes and/or evaluate others and events). • **Plus illustration** (you provide specific examples of what lead you to a particular attribute or evaluation) • **Plus inquiry** (you check out the adequacy of your views or thinking with others)	**You say why you think it** (rather than believe in the absolute correctness of your views and as a result provide no reason for why you hold them) 'I raise this for discussion because I think Running Record Analysis links nicely with our services emphasis on functional assessment.'	• It is likely that interpersonal relationships and group dynamics will be perceived as being minimally defensive. • It is likely that there will be frequent public testing of 'theories', views and inferences.

To enhance commitment and responsibility for monitoring the effectiveness of any choices made	Protection of self is a joint enterprise and oriented towards learning and growth. ⏎⏎ The protection of others, including difficult or emotional-charged issues is a bilateral task.	***Inquiry*** (you publicly test the adequacy of your views and others views and understandings – critique and inquire ***for valid information***) ⏎⏎ ***You publicly check out your understanding with others*** (rather than not checking and expecting others to know what you think). ⏎ 'I was wondering whether you had thought about this.' ⏎⏎ ***You embed dialogue within an interpersonal style***, which increases the likelihood that others will listen and not choose to become defensive.	• It is likely that learning-oriented norms will be perceived as being important. ⏎ • It is likely that problem-solving effectiveness will be increased through the greater availability and quality of information produced. ⏎ • It is likely that double-loop learning norms develop. ⏎ • It is likely that participants will perceive a high freedom of choice, internal commitment and increased risk taking. ⏎ • It is likely that any substantive emotional issues will be discussed and will not jeopardise problem-solving effectiveness.

Although Michelle and Mandy communicated, it was neither satisfactory nor constructive for either party. The interaction concluded with Michelle feeling that she had not achieved her goal of providing Mandy with 'clear and frank' feedback and, now feels that their relationship is likely to deteriorate further. Mandy, on the other hand, has been left confused and bemused, as she is still unsure as to the real purpose of the meeting and what Michelle's issues really are. Mandy believes she has been doing what has been expected of her. She is unsure why things appear to have escalated, why Michelle could not explain clearly what the issues were and as a result, she feels confused and uncomfortable.

So, despite communication having occurred with an implicit agenda on Michelle's part, it would appear that key features were absent within their interaction.

Key theoretical ideas and concepts

Argyris and Schön (1974, 1996) spent many hours and years video- and audio-recording the manner in which people went about the task of communicating and problem-solving together. On the basis of an analysis of subsequent transcripts and debriefings with people they formulated a model to guide more effective communication (Model II or Accessible Dialogue).

Central to this model is the notion of **Theories of Action** (Argyris and Schön, 1974, 1996, see Figure 5.1). These are the tacit underlying beliefs and values that implicitly guide our communications from one context to another. As human beings we strive for consistency, so, unless we can accurately deduce what our theories of action are, decide if we can live with them or aim to alter them to produce new outcomes, we are destined to replicate our typical ways of acting, despite our best intentions.

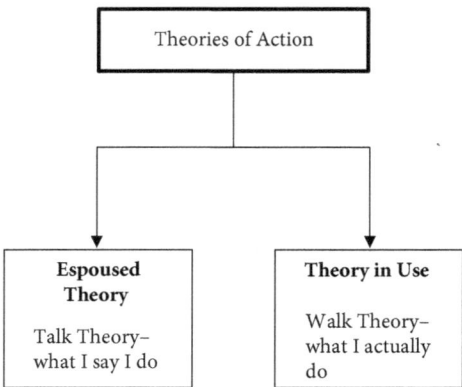

Figure 5.1 Two types of Theories of Action (after Argyris and Schön, 1974).

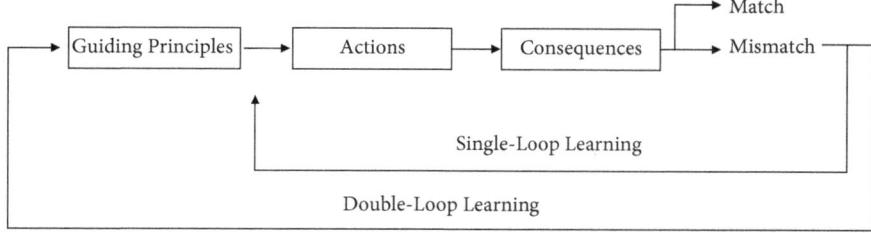

Figure 5.2 Single- and double-loop learning.
Source: Adapted from Robinson, Viviane (2018). Reduce Change to Increase Improvement. Corwin: Sage. Figure 2.4, page 21.

Argyris and Schön (1974, 1996) developed a means of evaluating such theories (Model I and Model II), ways for people to identify their **Theories in Use** (what people actually do and say) and importantly strategies (Model II or Accessible Dialogue) that will enable people to identify, test and take personal responsibility for their new ways of thinking and acting (double loop rather than single-loop learning). (Argyris and Schön, 1974, 1996; Robinson, 1993, 2014, 2018).

Reflexive questions

1. Have you ever tried to change something about yourself?
2. How effective was it?
3. What things helped you change?
4. What things may have prevented you from changing?

Theories of Action – Espoused Theories of Action (what I say I do and why) versus Theories in Use (what I actually do and say)

Given Lichtenberg's (1997) cautions that experience alone will not be sufficient to improve communication skills, as a teacher you need to therefore be able to:

- critically reflect upon our own thinking and behaviour, and
- ask yourself 'what did I think I was aiming to do or achieve (what was the purpose or goal of a particular encounter)?'; 'what actually occurred?' and 'can I live with the match or mismatch between what I thought would happen and what actually occurred?'

Michelle and Mandy engaged in a communication that represented an outward expression of their internal or tacit personal Theories of Action about how to communicate and interact with others, to understand and achieve their goals or purposes.

Within Theories of Action Argyris and Schön (1974, 1996) make a critical distinction between **Espoused Theories** versus **Theories of Use** (see Figure 5.1). Espoused Theories of Action are what people say they did and why they did it, and are referred to as 'talk theories'. Theories of Use are the actual strategies deployed during an interaction, and are referred to as 'walk theories' (Robinson, 2018).

Both types have the same tripartite structure as detailed in Figure 5.2, namely the actions that occurred, in this case the **Communication Strategies**, the beliefs and values that gave rise to those actions, referred to here as **Guiding Principles** and the intended and unintended **Consequences** of those beliefs and actions (Argyris and Schön, 1974, 1996; Robinson, 2018).

Espoused Theories are based on reports of what you have done or intended to do while, Theories of Use are inferred from records (video- or audio-recorded), or observations and notes of what actually happened. If the two parties did exactly what they intended their theory in use would match their espoused theory.

In the case study, Michelle's espoused theory of what had occurred would match that of Mandy. Mandy would be clear about what Michelle's concerns were, the examples used to illustrate them and would have been able to communicate her own perspectives. They would have reached a consensus of what the concerns were (based on valid and accurate evidence that both could agree upon) and what needed to change, and how.

Given that we cannot directly observe the beliefs and values that drive our own or others behaviour, it is important to acknowledge that revealing a theory-in-use involves making inferences about others beliefs and values, and how they lead to the actions and consequences observed (Robinson, 2018).

If you want to reduce the gap between what you thought you were doing and what actually occurred, it is a good idea to clarify the underlying beliefs and values that informed the behaviour and its intended and unintended consequences. For change to occur we need to target not the behaviour, but the underlying theories that sustain those actions (Robinson, 2018).

You can get such feedback as part of your professional development by recording selective communications (with permission, and following agreed protocols for such work) and using this in supervision or coaching to explore what your own theories of action might be (see Chapter 1 for more information on the coaching model). You are then in a much better position to identify what maintains your existing communication style (behaviours) and what might be involved in changing them over time, to get different and more effective outcomes.

Teaching is a busy and demanding profession, so the motivation to exert such effort to look critically at your own actions, what sustains them and their consequences emerges from real feelings of dissatisfaction with the outcomes of some of your communications with others. This is the starting point of a realization that things did not go as planned, or were uncomfortable – it is the 'hairs rising on the back of our neck' moment!

> **Reflective questions**
>
> 1. Think of times when you have felt annoyed during a conversation, what thoughts and feelings were going through your head?
> 2. What did you do to try and manage the situation?
> 3. Did it work?

These are likely to be similar to the feelings that Michelle and Mandy experienced following their conversation. These feelings may well be dismissed, especially by Michelle who is in a power relationship over Mandy and may feel she is right, by mere fact of her positional role. But, even in Michelle's case if she is having too many of these types of encounters it is likely that things will not go as she had planned and eventually a need for doing things differently may arise.

From Michelle's perspective her espoused theory as opposed to her theory-of-use was that she needed to provide Mandy with clear feedback on things that were annoying her. Yet, this is an assumption, as at no point did she publically check out with Mandy that they both had a shared understanding of why she had called the meeting, what the issues were, supported with valid evidence (from her perspective, of course) and including Mandy's perspectives and examples. She assumed Mandy would implicitly understand and would therefore agree and change in the ways she wanted her to. This is sometimes referred to as 'magical thinking'!

Sadly, these are all untested assumptions and it is highly unlikely that Mandy will change because she does not understand what she needs to do differently and why, or indeed if they are valid criticisms. Mandy is likely to feel defensive when talking with Michelle in the future, potentially further stressing an already uncomfortable relationship. Paradoxically, Mandy's behaviour will merely reinforce for Michelle her untested assumptions and attributions, and a vicious cycle will likely develop.

Single- and double-loop learning

Michelle has decided that she is unhappy with the mismatch between what she thought she was doing when she was talking with Mandy, what actually happened and some of the unintended consequences. There are two types of action learning – single- and double-loop learning (Argyris and Schön, 1974, 1996) (see Figure 5.2). In single loop learning we intuitively strive to maintain the status quo, so although we may make changes, they are designed in such a way as to not conflict with our existing Guiding Principles (beliefs and values).

A good example of the model in practice can be seen in the work of the London-based charities, Christian Solidarity International and the Bridge Child Care Consultancy, with the Moscow social services in attempting to manage the problem of 'street children' in Russia's capital city. Since many of these young people had been brought up in Children's Homes (where they had acquired institutional-specific skills, which often prevented them from obtaining or holding down a regular job) early attempts to manage this problem focused on the state-run Children's Homes and other institutions with a view to minimizing their 'institutional' effects (this is a single-loop learning solution). However, a more recent examination of the beliefs which underpinned the existence of Children's Homes and linking with research on attachment and parenting (a double-loop learning approach) has led to the setting up of the country's first training schemes for potential foster 'parents' whose care may prevent children coming into homes in the first place. These actions may lead to a different and more positive set of outcomes (Cameron and Monsen, 1998).

An issue with many teachers is that to have achieved what they have, they are less likely to have experienced failure. Because of this, and paradoxically, when working with pupils who come in all shapes and sizes, they may not have 'learned to learn' from failure experiences. So, whenever one's intuitive single-loop strategies do not work, people may choose to become defensive, censor criticism and locate the 'blame' away from themselves. Ironically, at the very time that a teacher needs to adopt a double-loop learning stance is the time when they shut down. It is highly likely that they are destined to repeat the same behaviours and experience, and the same intended and unintended consequences again and again.

Accessible dialogue for teachers – learning how to reason productively key components

Despite the real cultural power of defensive reasoning, teachers are motivated to act in a way that is consistent with what they intended. This contributes to a sense of professional competency and beliefs about themselves as being a 'good and competent teacher'.

The position of this chapter is that teachers can be taught how to clarify the reasoning which they use to design and implement their actions (verbal behaviour). Teachers can be helped to identify the inconsistencies between their espoused and actual theories of action. They can acknowledge the fact that they intuitively design and execute actions that they do not intend. Finally, teachers can learn to collect valid data on their actions, analyse it carefully and constantly test the inferences drawn from it, in a cycle of personal development.

The next section takes the Accessible Dialogue framework, as presented in Table 5.2, and explains each of the five columns so that you can learn to use the approach. Table 5.1 presents Model I by way of contrast, and both can be used when analysing communications. In this way you can identify what strategies you are currently using and what might underpin these. You can then design different strategies and test these out seeing what consequences are subsequently generated.

Column 1 – Guiding principles (underlying beliefs and values)

Accessible Dialogue is based upon three core guiding principles. When you are communicating with others for the first time or when you feel there might be misunderstandings you are aiming to:

- Increase valid information for you and others so that communication and problem-solving effectiveness are improved.
- Maximize the production of valid information. This means that you provide the other person with direct, observable data and correct reporting and/or accounts of what they are talking about (rather than untested attributions or assumptions), so they can make valid attributions about themselves and others.
- Enhance free and informed choice to any agreement or understanding reached. Choice, in this sense, is the degree that the individual feels that they can define their own objectives; define how to achieve these; define them within their current capabilities; and relate their objectives to general personal needs. The individual feels that they themselves are responsible for their choices.

Column 2 – What kind of interpersonal environment is likely to be co-created

It is likely that by adopting these guiding principles you will engender the following dynamics.

- You will experience a high degree of personal autonomy and causation.
- The dialogue and its tasks will be jointly managed.
- The protection of self will be a joint enterprise and orientated towards learning and growth.
- The protection of others, including difficult or emotionally charged issues will be a bilateral task.

You and the other person are encouraged to speak and use directly observable categories, rather than making great inferential leaps (which assume that your view or theirs is self-evident). In this way, tentative hypotheses can be carefully tested and checked out with the other person. This avoids the possibility of misunderstanding or conflict. One of the key characteristics of accessible dialogue theory-in-use is the emphasis it places upon empirical data or 'facts'. An example might be, 'Thank you for letting me observe you lesson today. I'd like to start by asking what was your rationale was for not using small groups for the follow-up activity to the whole class input?'

You and the other person will publicly test the assumptions of their theory-in-use and be open to the possibilities for change in their own behaviour that may result from such testing. Attributions will be formed openly on the basis of directly, observable data. An example might be, 'Thank you for meeting with me to discuss the literacy strategy. When you said in your email that there is no extra money to set up a whole school paired reading programme, did this also mean the use of grandparent readers?'

Enabling the production and sharing of valid information makes dilemmas of practice recognizable. This creates the cognitive tension required to resolve them. Learning, in this sense, is based on the discovery and surfacing of dilemmas.

Column 3 – Communication strategies employed in the behavioural world

In looking at the behavioural strategies used during communication, we observe people advocating their own ideas and opinions. Within an Accessible Dialogue, **advocacy** (making your views, the reasoning behind them and their fallibility explicit to the other person) can be expressed in three ways.

- **With an illustration** (you share specific evidenced examples of what you mean and are talking about);
- **With your reasoning** (you share your theory about these events in such a way which enables them to be tested out);
- **With open enquiry** (you check out with others regarding the adequacy of your views and theories).

In addition to advocacy, we can observe people making **inferences** (you infer certain attributes and/or evaluate others and events). Within the Accessible Dialogue framework inferences can be expressed in two ways.

- **With an illustration** (you provide specific examples of what led you to a particular attribute or evaluation);
- **With open enquiry** (you check out the adequacy of your views or thinking with others).

Enquiry, in both cases, is undertaken to publically test out the adequacy of your views and understandings as well as the other person. Such critique and enquiry are undertaken to produce valid information.

You can use these categories (for Model I, people still advocate and infer but they do not illustrate, reason or inquiry) to code the transcript of your dialogue. In this way you are building up an understanding of what you are currently doing and its impact or effect on others.

Column 4 – Illustrations and examples and Column 5 – Consequences for learning

The Accessible Dialogue approach can be summed up as:

1. **You say** what **you think** within the terms of your professional relationship with the other person(s), rather than hide what you think and, operate as if it was self-evident and correct.

Consequences:

- It is likely that you and the other person will be perceived as being minimally defensive. This is likely to increase the opportunities that honest views and opinions will be publically shared, thus increase the availability of accurate information.
- It is likely that you and the other person will perceive that any hidden agendas are actually open to debate, discussion and critique.
- It is likely that you and the other person will perceive higher degrees of openness and trust.

2. **You say** why **you think** it rather than believe in the absolute correctness of your views, and as a result provide no reason for why you hold them.

Consequences:

- It is likely that there will be frequent public testing of theories, views and inferences.

3. **You publicly** check out your understanding with others rather than not checking and expecting others to know what you think.

Consequences:

- It is likely that learning orientated norms will be perceived as being important.
- It is likely that problem-solving effectiveness will be increased due to the greater availability and quality of information produced.
- It is likely that double-loop learning norms will develop.

4. You embed the dialogue with an interpersonal style which increases the likelihood that others will listen and not choose to become defensive.

Consequences:

- It is likely that you and the other person will perceive a high freedom of personal choice, internal commitment and increased risk-taking.
- It is likely that any substantive emotional issues discussed will not jeopardise problem-solving effectiveness.

Summary

Viviane Robinson's (1998a, b) guidelines for conducting a learning conversation provide an excellent summary of the essential skills underpinning the Accessible Dialogue process.

Think. Reflect about why you are concerned or unsettled about the problem you have encountered or are experiencing. Clarify your theory of action: espoused theory, theory-in-use. What is your theory of action based upon? Clarify the constraints of the situation. Work out how you are going to say what you now think to the other person and why you think it ('I have noticed Mandy that you seem to spend a lot of your time with the more able pupils. I am motivated to make sure that the less able pupils also get a fair proportion of your time as well').

Say. State your views honestly ('Mandy I noticed that you do not seem to explain to the groups what they have to do after my input. I am worried that this might explain why they take a while to get started on the activities. What do you think about that?'). Express clearly to the other person why you think this way. Find out how the other person thinks and feels about the issue. Actively seek feedback from the other person.

Listen. Listen very carefully to the other person's response and watch their non-verbal behaviours. Assist the other person to express their views ('Would you like to tell me more about what you were thinking when I asked you that question which seemed to annoy you?').

Check. Actively check out your understanding of the other person's views and reactions. You could paraphrase to clarify your interpretations ('So you are saying that you got annoyed with my question because the concerns had never been raised before and you were taken aback').

Collaborate. After issues have been raised and views have been expressed and clarified, encourage active, and constructive collaboration about how to deal with what has been discovered ('What do you need from me? How can we work together on this?').

Concluding remarks

Next steps in learning Accessible Dialogue

In terms of your ongoing professional development the key characteristics are:

- Actively working towards obtaining valid information about your effectiveness;
- Aiming for as little inconsistency between your espoused theory and between your theory-in-use as you can live with;
- Working at contributing to an environment that produces valid information about each other's espoused theory, theory-in-use and any inconsistencies within each theory as well as among them.

The best place to make a start is to choose the relatively safe context of a role-play with a colleague. Explain to them that you are wanting to improve your interpersonal communication skills and that you want their help.

Afterwards as a courtesy ask your colleague for what they liked and did not like so much about the encounter but stress from the outset that they refer to actual dialogue and examples ('when you said "there was … no time to discuss the programme …" I was thinking in my head "so that's it then" not open to exploration. I must admit I was annoyed at that point and this affected my later responses to you').

Often, as part of automatic defensive routines discussed earlier, people disclose that their behaviour during a role-play bears little resemblance to what they would do in real life.

This is usually said when things might not have gone as planned publically. Given the arguments shared earlier, human beings are surprisingly consistent in their actions unless they change their core beliefs and values – role-plays can be a valid and accurate analogue of actual real-world interactions and useful for learning and trying out new things in a safe environment.

Ask permission to record the role-play (video-recording is fine but it introduces added complexity around body language and personal demeanour. At this stage, we are interested in verbal behaviour). Having an accurate record of what was said is useful, because you can spend your time focused on the other person rather than having to make notes. You can re-play it to yourself and select segments to play to your supervisor of what you felt went well (and why, with your rationale) and also what were less successful segments (and why, with your rationale). Usually five minutes is more than sufficient to get a good sample to work on.

Before the role-play, it is important to brief your colleague about who they will be playing, and your role. Having a one-page bullet point scenario can aid this process. It is useful to have given some thought beforehand and draw upon a recent encounter, where you felt things had not gone to plan (feeding back to a parent/carer at parents evening; giving feedback to your linked learning support assistant; meeting the educational and child psychologist following an observation in your classroom).

After the role-play, and when you are ready, fold some paper vertically producing two columns – the left-hand side will detail a verbatim transcript of segments of the tape recorded interaction (It is surprisingly easy to do this) and the right-hand side is your analysis (using the concepts shared on Accessible Dialogue and Model I, as contrast). Do not be surprised that in the early stages your actions seem to conform more to Model I strategies. Given our socialization most of us operate in this way unless we consciously attempt to act differently.

Tables 5.1 and 5.2 can be used to structure and inform your analysis drawing upon some of the key concepts. So for example, in the case study shared earlier:

Michelle – The reason I wanted to meet with you was to check out how you think things are going in the classroom? As you know, I only started in September and it's been a really busy term. [Michelle was certainly advocating why she wanted to meet with Mandy but it was minus – illustration, reasoning and inquiring. She assumed that Mandy understood and would provide the views she had in her own head. This was probably done to avoid emotions and raising what could be seen as critical views – so this could be coded *Advocacy Minus Inquiry, Minus Reasoning and Minus Inquiry*. We would want Michelle to try out the opening introduction that made her thinking and rationale for meeting much clearer and for her to stop and check in with Mandy that she was both clear and could also offer her own views and perspectives].

You can now identify some learning goals and aim to practise these, initially in the safe context of a role-play but as soon as possible during real-world encounters. Michelle aimed to work at opening comments that set the scene for the communication by being clearer about her agenda for meeting and checking this out with Mandy.

Michelle – Thank you for meeting up with me today Mandy. As you know we have been working together now for over a term. During that time we have developed ways of working together. I thought as the new term was approaching that it would be useful for both of us to take stock and reflect upon our working approaches and agree what was working well. I'd also like to explore and check out with you two examples of where I feel we need to do things differently. Is that a helpful way of structuring our review and did you have anything to add or change? [Michelle was certainly advocating why she wanted to meet with Mandy and this time it was shared with – plus illustration, plus reasoning and plus inquiring].

In your analysis try and stick as closely as possible to the observable verbal behaviour. With your supervisor's help, try to:

- look forward and predict possible consequences of such behaviour on yourself, the other person and the interpersonal environment created.

- look backward and try to identify what could be the guiding principles (beliefs and values) that supported such behaviour.
- identify possible constraints in your thinking that may make you resistant to change or taking a risk and testing out new way of doing things.

When you begin to design new behaviour based upon your analysis and goals, the same three steps are useful for learning about the consequences and the effectiveness of your new behaviour.

Ultimately, the process should be a solution-generating one based upon an accurate analysis of valid information. It is important to stress that at first you may experience discomfort and begin to feel discouraged which may lead to you either giving up or choosing less effective strategies. The key is to learn to live with this discomfort and work through it, with the support of your supervisor.

Implications for you as a teacher

1. Search for inconsistencies based upon accurate and valid information.
2. Explore new models to reduce the inconsistencies identified and increase your effectiveness.
3. Test new behaviours publicly (but tentatively). Depending upon the results of the test you might loop back through steps one and two.
4. If the new behaviour is effective, internalize and feel responsible for it (Argyris and Schön, 1974).

Reflective questions

1. What are the three big ideas you take from this chapter?
2. What aspects of your communications style do you want to work on, and why?
3. How are you going to make it happen?

Window on research

Interpersonal decision-making and problem-solving communication

Slotte, S. and Hämäläinen, R. P. (2015). 'Decision structuring dialogue'. *EURO Journal on Decision Processes*, 3(1–2), pp. 141–59.

Slotte and Hämäläinen (2015) present a group decision-making dialogue method called decision structuring dialogue (DSD), which aims to collectively facilitate the structuring and framing of complex problems within groups who have conflicting interests. The DSD aims to do this by focusing on the conversational aspect of problem-solving, by facilitating group dialogue during challenging decision-making, to help the group to create alternative decisions and to reach a shared view of the problem. Slotte and Hämäläinen tested the DSD on a group of individuals who had conflicting views regarding a Finnish lake regulation project. The DSD is suitable for structuring problems within a group of individuals who hold conflicting views and multiple perspectives. The participants felt that the main problem that they wanted to rectify involved the difficulties surrounding the trust and communication in the group. The authors found that the method was applied successfully, and that the dialogue helped members of the group to talk about and frame the problem in a constructive way. Furthermore, the method received positive feedback, with group members agreeing that the method helped group members to respect each other's differing view points and enabled decisions to be made using common ground. Furthermore, all group members agreed that they would use the dialogue framework in future discussions regarding the regulation of the lake, suggesting that the DSD has practical implications.

This study has numerous links with Accessible Dialogue and shows the importance of verbal communications, structuring problem-solving processing and enabling all participants to share their perspectives, so that a group consensus based upon evidence can be achieved.

Annotated bibliography

Arygris, C. and Schön, D. A. (1974). *Theory into practice.* **San Francisco, CA: Jossey-Bass.**
This is the book that started the whole exploration of Theories in Action and greatly influenced people like Robinson. It is written in an accessible and engaging style and is one of those books that you can dip in and out of. It addresses many of the areas that are touched upon in this chapter in much greater detail and so makes an ideal companion to those that want to learn Accessible Dialogue.

Robinson, V. (2018). *Reduce change to increase improvement.* **Corwin, CA: Sage.**
This book is of relevance to every teacher who is serious about educational change in their classroom and/or school. In this evidence-based book Robinson uses many of the ideas explored in this chapter to critically focus on the impact that teachers have on children/young people's learning. Robinson stresses that only by integrating new ways of thinking about your own classroom practice will real lasting change be sustained. This is achieved in part by openly sharing tacit beliefs about the capacity of all pupils to learn.

6
Resilience, Reflection and Reflexivity
James Boyle and Elizabeth N. King

A toast by Sir William Curtis, Lord Mayor of London, to 'The three Rs – Reading, Writing and Rithmetic' (Timbs, 1825, p. 461) is one of the earliest references to the traditional understanding of the core skills of education required to participate in the workplace, and indeed wider society. This approach emphasized the knowledge-base of the school curriculum but has been superseded by an understanding of the importance for pupils of 'twenty-first-century skills' such as critical thinking, meta-cognitive, learning, interpersonal, communication and technological skills allied to creativity and collaboration (Ananiadou and Claro, 2009; Partnership for 21st century learning, 2007).

Some approaches link twenty-first-century skills and attributes associated with effective pupil learning with a framework of the 'new' Three Rs (see Burns, 2008; Sternberg, 2008; Wagner et al., 2006). But teachers also require the skills, personal qualities and characteristics to cope with the challenges and demands of schools and classrooms. Further, they also need to develop their knowledge of the curriculum and their subject areas. In this chapter, we will focus upon what psychological theory and research can tell us about resilience, reflection and reflexivity. How might these help you to understand teachers' lived-in professional experience? To what extent might they constitute a 'New Three Rs' for teachers?

Understanding resilience

With its long days, intensive social engagement with pupils, and high levels of marking and administration, teaching can be a stressful job (for a review see Castle and Buckler, 2018). Teachers are often being asked to do more with less, and are subject to the pressures of competing demands, high levels of expectations and accountability, as evidenced by 'burnout' and 'exit' rates. Recent surveys in the UK reveal disquieting levels of poor mental health and well-being amongst teachers, with some 65 per cent of respondents reporting that they experience high levels of occupational stress attributed to heavy workloads, problems with pupil behaviour in class, concerns about resources and lack of support from senior colleagues (Education Support Partnership, 2018; OFSTED, 2019) (see also Chapter 2).

The ability to cope with adverse circumstances and stress is referred to as 'resilience', more formally defined as 'as reduced vulnerability to environmental risk experiences, the overcoming of a stress or adversity, or a relatively good outcome despite risk experiences' (Rutter, 2012, p. 336). Resilience is often conceptualized in tandem with the levels of 'risk' associated with adverse experience (Rutter, 2000). So how might you best understand the concept? Firstly, as Rutter (2012) points out, it is an inference, drawn from evidence, be it observation, self-report or report by significant others, of a positive outcome to an adverse, negative experience. Secondly, there is considerable individual variation in resilience which has given rise to research into risk and protective factors and the role of genetic and environmental aspects, as well as the role of 'strengths', such as self-efficacy, which was discussed in Chapter 2.

Reflective questions

1. Should we conceptualize resilience as a 'trait', a stable constitutional or personality characteristic which is resistant to change and which an individual either has or does not have?
2. As a more fluid 'capacity' which might increase through experience and perhaps intervention?
3. As the effective use of coping strategies?
4. As an interactive process which takes into account both genetic and environmental factors?
5. In terms of tapping into strengths and positive qualities such as optimism, hope, and self-efficacy, to take responsibility only for factors within one's control, and to integrate and make sense of experiences?

Reflexive question

To what extent might the concept of resilience encourage explanations of the effects of stress which 'blame' the teacher struggling to cope with high levels of workload and demands while minimizing the effects of underfunding and under-resourcing within the education system?

To consider these issues we now turn to psychological theories which address 'resilience'.

Attachment theory

Early research and theories of resilience have their roots in the 'mental hygiene movement' and sought to account for individual differences in the outcomes of children's experience of stress and adverse childhood events, such as maternal deprivation, attachment and loss, parental/caregiver mental illness, violence within the home, fostering and adoption, living in children's homes, as well as physical, emotional and sexual abuse (Rutter, 2000).

'Attachment theory' introduced in the 1950s by the psychiatrist John Bowlby links individual differences in the long-term mental health of children and young people who have experienced stress and adversity to the quality of their parenting and childcare (Bowlby, 1969, 1982). The theory has informed major clinical interventions as well as decision-making and child-care policies throughout the world. It continues to be an important area of research for developmental and educational psychologists as well as other clinicians (see Simpson and Rholes, 2015; Sutton, 2019).

Attachment theory has its focus on the impact of the child's relationships in the early years with their primary caregivers (identified as 'mothers' in early reports, with fathers and other carers taken into account in later publications) on subsequent emotional and mental health problems in childhood and in adulthood. It also has an emphasis upon representation and object relations theory (Bowlby, 1982). Further, the theory takes an evolutionary approach to socio-emotional development informed by insights for the survival of species drawn from animal studies, including observations of imprinting and other parent–offspring behaviour in the wild and laboratory studies of maternal deprivation and separation in rhesus monkeys (Bowlby, 1982).

Attachment is distinctive from 'bonding' (see Brody, 1981), and is defined by Bowlby (1969, p. 194) as a 'lasting psychological connectedness between human beings', a connectedness which is strengthened by behaviours that cause the infant to become closely related to the primary caregiver and which can have an effect upon the course and character of the child's relationships with others across the developmental lifespan. Consistent positive attachment relationships with primary caregivers and significant others are prerequisites for the child's mental health and social and emotional development. The attachment relationship between child and parents/carers begins during pregnancy and develops over the first three years of life leading to increased emotional security and independence.

Attachments develop through relationship-specific 'Internal Working Models' (IWMs). These are cognitive–emotive structures based on experience of relationships, initially with primary caregivers, which direct future behaviour throughout the individual's lifespan. IWMs do this through the development of the mental representations required by the individual at both the cognitive level (planning, reflection and prediction) and the emotional level (for understanding their lived experience, relationships, expectations and awareness of the perspectives of others, as well as the impact of these upon feelings of self-worth).

As 'states of mind', IWMs cannot be directly observed, but are inferred from children's behaviours in tasks such as the 'Strange Situation' (Ainsworth et al., 1978) where infants are placed in three stressful situations in a clinical setting involving the infant, the caregiver and a stranger. Ainsworth and colleagues identified three distinctive attachment 'styles', each with a related IWM: 'secure', 'insecure-avoidant' and 'insecure-ambivalent' (see Bunce and Rickards, 2004 for details).

A fourth attachment style, 'insecure disorganized' was later identified by Main and Solomon (1990) and describes the most serious and unpredictable inconsistency in parenting. The IWM here is derived from experiences of affection but also of neglect, perhaps even of aggression, which leads to high levels of stress and long-term problems in relationships and resilience.

Attachment styles are widely used in clinical settings for assessment, and research indicates cross-cultural differences, with variations linked to expectations of child independence and child-rearing practice (Mesmer et al., 2016).

Researchers have studied the attachment styles of adults, using instruments such as the 'Adult Attachment Interview' (AAI) (Steele and Steele, 2008). This is a semi-structured interview which asks adult participants to describe the childhood memories of attachment with parents and other primary caregivers and has three categories for scoring: 'secure-autonomous', 'insecure-dismissing' and 'insecure preoccupied'. Those in the 'secure' category can evaluate their own experiences of attachment (be they positive or negative) and highly value attachment relationships and are aware of their importance. Those in the 'insecure-dismissing' category place less value on the importance of attachment for their own lives or may have an unrealistically positive evaluation of their own childhood attachment experience without being able to give specific examples. Finally, adults in the 'insecure preoccupied' category are either very passive, or perhaps express anger about their childhood experiences.

A literature review of the findings from the AAI revealed that over 40 per cent of combined samples of mothers from non-clinical US and European studies reported some degree of insecure attachments (Bakermans-Kranenburg and van IJzendoorn, 2009). This is of further interest in the light of research which reveals that parents' own history of relationships and of the attachment styles they have experienced themselves can influence the quality of relationships both with other adults and with their children. IWMs are used to explain this phenomenon of 'treating their children as they were treated themselves', the 'intergenerational transmission' of parents' IWM through their transactional relationships with the children (Howe, 1995).

Attachment theory has a strong research base which accounts for resilience in terms of attachment style and quality of relationships with caregivers. The connection between early attachment experiences and life outcomes is based upon a complex interplay between attachment experience, the child's environment, parental sensitivity or even maltreatment, and the processes of general development. Those who experience secure attachment are held to be better able to cope with adverse experiences than those who endured insecure or disorganized attachment. Further, as each relationship is held to have a separate IWM, a supportive and responsive teacher may help to foster within the child a secure sense of self, even if this is unavailable at home. While attachment theory and the stability of attachment style have been criticized (see Harlow, 2019; Stern et al., 2018; Vicedo, 2017), Riley (2011) argues that an understanding of IWM can provide teachers with an insight into the IWM of their pupils. By reflecting on their own IWM, teachers can better understand classroom interactions and use these insights to more effectively manage interactions and behaviour within the classroom. In this way, as well as accounting for individual differences in resilience, attachment theory may help to shape our understanding of what it means to be a teacher who 'makes a difference' (Cozolino, 2013; Pajares and Urdan, 2008).

Reflective questions

1. How would you recognize whether a pupil has a secure attachment?
2. How might you support a pupil with an insecure attachment?

Reflexive questions

1. How important is it to understand your own attachment style?
2. How might teachers find out more about their IWMs of attachment?

Research reveals links between the classification of attachment styles and levels of stress hormones in young children, with disorganized attachment relationships associated with highest levels of stress and secure attachments with the lowest levels (Fong et al., 2017). The lower levels of stress associated with secure attachment have been observed to have an impact upon the development of the right hemisphere of the child's brain which in turn is associated with development of coping strategies (Schore, 2001), to which we now turn.

Cognitive theories: Transactional coping theory and resilience

Coping strategies are processes used by individuals to deal with stressors and stressful situations in adversity and hence underpin the individual's resilience. One of the most influential models of coping is the transactional theory developed by Lazarus and Folkman (1984) (see also McCarthy, 2019). This is a cognitive model which identifies two broad categories of coping strategy. The first, 'problem-focused', involves the use of adaptive strategies such as problem-solving, help-seeking or support-seeking to reduce the experience of stress. The second, 'emotion-focused', involves the use of less adaptive strategies such as wishful thinking, helplessness or escape which are focused on regulation of the emotional responses to the stressors to reduce feelings of anxiety without doing anything directly to tackle the stressors.

The theory holds that 'problem-focused' and 'emotion-focused' strategies are selected by means of 'appraisal' processes which reflect 'person' variables, such as the age and gender of the individual, and 'situation-specific' variables, such as the nature and severity of stressful encounters. There are two types of appraisal process: 'primary' (based upon the meaning attributed to the stressful event, for example as a *threat* because a negative outcome is anticipated or as a *challenge* because positive outcomes are expected) and 'secondary' (based upon feelings related to the stress in the light of an evaluation of the coping strategies available in specific situations, such as a perception of *controllability*). These two processes are not exclusive and both could be utilized in selecting a coping strategy.

The processes of appraisal and coping can account for how a teacher experiencing stress from, for example, classroom behaviour issues from pupils, might deal effectively with the stressors. Primary appraisal processes could reframe the issues as a challenge rather than a threat (and an opportunity to further develop professional skills in positive behaviour management), and secondary appraisal processes could indicate sufficient resources and control to deal with the situation. Such appraisals would lend themselves to the teacher 'owning the problem' and the selection of problem-focused coping strategies including seeking support from colleagues.

In contrast, if the teacher's primary appraisals of the stressors were as a threat and their secondary appraisals indicated insufficient resources to deal with the problem, then this could result in the selection of emotion-focused coping strategies such as withdrawal or avoidance of dealing with the situation, which would be less adaptive.

Hunter and Boyle (2004) examine in detail how the transactional theory of coping can account for dealing with stress drawing upon experiences of bullying and victimization. At a more general level, Skinner and Saxton (2019) report the findings from a systematic review of sixty-six studies of dealing with academic stress. These highlight the importance for teachers and pupils alike of personal resources (self-worth, autonomy, motivation, belonging and engagement) and interpersonal resources (e.g. support from parents, teachers and peers) in coping with stress.

Biosocial models: Risk, protective factors and resilience

'Biosocial' models (Rutter, 2000, 2006, 2012) conceptualize individual differences in coping with adversity in terms of 'risk' and 'protective' factors. They represent a move away from the emphasis upon 'person-focused' views of resilience characteristic of attachment theory to 'variable-focused' conceptualizations of resilience at the levels of systems such as families, schools, classrooms and peer groups more generally. These allow the exploration of contributions not only of the quality of parenting, but also of wider family dynamics and importantly, of how these interact with the underlying processes which regulate the child's emotions, learning and behaviour to account for individual differences in resilience in the face of adversity. This is reflected in broader understandings of resilience as 'positive patterns of adaptation in the context of adversity' (Masten and Obradovic, 2006, p. 14) and of adversity as 'negative contexts and experiences that have the potential to challenge adaptive functioning and development' (Yates et al., 2015, p. 774).

Rutter (2000) points out that much of the research into risk and protective factors is based upon two research paradigms: longitudinal studies of children, parents and adults over time; and studies comparing twins with adopted children, which provide information about genetic influences upon behaviour. Longitudinal studies reveal the importance of *positive turning points* (where support from peers or stable long-term partnership relationships can transform a negative life trajectory to a more adaptive, positive trajectory) and *indirect chain effects*. These effects account for research findings which reveal that while experiences or behaviour at an early stage associated with protective factors may predispose the individual to positive effects upon behaviour and development, in contrast, experiences associated with risk factors may predispose the individual to negative outcomes. However, while some children experience significant mental health issues as a result of adverse experiences, others appear more able to cope with similar adversity. These are referred to as strengthening or '*steeling*' events (Rutter, 2012) and are associated with brief exposures to situations where the levels of stress are considered manageable by the child, and result in self-efficacy and associated coping. A further related phenomenon is *stress buffering*, whereby protective factors buffer the effects of stress, for example, positive social support from colleagues in school, or high levels of motivation and self-efficacy in coping with classroom behaviour.

Research informed by biosocial models in this way has explored direct and unidirectional effects as well as the impact of co-occurring risk factors. This is done by studying the effects of *moderators* (variables that affect the size or direction of the effect of a predictor upon outcome measures of interest) and *mediators* (variables which account for the nature of the relationship between predictors and outcome measures, for example, a direct relationship with no mediation, or an indirect relationship, mediated by a predictor variable) (Baron and Kenny, 1986; Rucker et al., 2011).

The earliest studies into biosocial models focused on the relationship between adversity and the development of mental health problems, while a second wave investigated underlying processes and mechanisms of risk (Rutter, 2000). A third wave, focused on intervention studies and research into positive outcomes and experiences, provided an evidence-base to shape policy in regard to prevention and helping individuals exposed to adversity. Finally, a fourth (and current) wave has linked the study of genetics and gene–environment interactions with findings from neuroscience regarding the impact of adverse experiences upon brain development, motor development and perceptual development (Rutter, 2012). This level of integration has been used to develop models to account for the reciprocal effects on brain functioning and motor skills of factors such as poor attachment, poor nutrition and malnutrition, and abuse in young children (Berger, 2015; Coan, 2008; Schaffer, 2006) and behavioural difficulties in older children (Booth et al., 2000).

The 'diathesis-stress model' (see Arnau-Soler et al., 2019) and the 'developmental cascades' model (Blair et al., 2015; Masten and Cicchetti, 2010; Masten et al., 2005) are examples of such frameworks which account for mental health problems in terms of gene–environment interaction effects. In the case of the former approach, individuals with a genetic or biological predisposition or vulnerability known as a 'diathesis' are more likely to experience mental health problems or a psychological disorder when they are exposed to significant levels of negative stress (Arnau-Soler et al., 2019). Gene–environment interactions in twin and adoption studies are important in controlling for the confounding role of parents, who not only transmit their genes to their children, but also determine their child's environment. Thus, at the level of the child, there may be an interaction between (a) a genetic susceptibility towards, for example, depression, and (b) the effects of poor parenting at an environmental level. But in turn, viewed from the level of the parents/carers, the poor quality of relationship with the child might itself be the result of a further gene–environment interaction.

In addition to specific genetic and physiological factors, a diathesis might entail cognitions or personality factors (Sigelman and Rider, 2012). The model has been used to explain how a genetic predisposition to depression in children might only be triggered by significant or chronic levels of negative stress, for example, resulting from social exclusion by peers (Gazelle and Ladd, 2003). Protective factors such as positive attachment to parents/carers, supportive peers and high levels of self-acceptance may help the individual to cope with stress. The model can also account for the mental health of teachers. To illustrate this, consider Melissa and Tony, two teachers of Year 4 pupils. Melissa has experienced positive, secure attachment relationships with her family and long-term partner. She is a highly motivated and committed teacher who is well-regarded by her pupils and colleagues and well-supported by her school's leaders, although she finds her workload demanding. In contrast, Tony had a troubled relationship with his mother and step-father and problems also in his adult relationships with partners. He has difficulties in classroom management and finds it hard to talk to his colleagues about them. He feels under pressure from his head teacher to deal with complaints from parents about bullying in his class. In the absence of Melissa's protective factors, Tony would be more likely to have difficulty in coping with stress and given an equivalent genetic risk of depression, more likely to experience mental health and well-being issues.

The 'developmental tasks' approach links pathways of development to notions of positive adaptation (Masten, 2011; Sroufe et al., 2005). For Masten (2011) and Sroufe et al. (2005), positive adaptation in development, or resilience, is determined by the extent to which the child experiences success in meeting age-appropriate developmental tasks which reflect the standards and social expectations of parents/carers, school and society, gender and culture. The successful resolution of early developmental tasks leads to positive adaptation which makes it more likely that subsequent tasks will be successfully resolved, resulting in continuity in development which is likely to be 'heterotypic' in nature, that is with behaviours reflecting the same processes although the form of the behaviours may change (Schaffer, 2006). However, if the development tasks are not successfully resolved, then this may have consequences for the child's adaptation and in turn for their resilience in coping with risk or adversity (Masten, 2011).

But what of risk and protective factors? The evidence from studies across the four waves of research in this area indicates that risk factors such as below-average levels of cognitive abilities; poor or negative attachments; low self-efficacy and self-regulation; poor family dynamics; negative peer group influences; and values which run counter to those of the individual's society and culture are associated with poor resilience and negative outcomes (Masten and Obradovic, 2006; Rutter, 2000). Following Rutter, protective factors in general may be conceptualized as the 'antonyms' of risk factors. Thus, the presence of average levels (or above) of cognitive abilities on the part of the individual; positive attachments with parents and caregivers and in adulthood with friends and life partners; high levels of self-efficacy and of self-regulation of both emotions and behaviour; positive family dynamics and appropriate expectations from family members and partners; positive peer group influences; and values and standards which are consistent with the norms and values of the individual's culture are all associated with resilient, adaptive behaviour and social competence and are in turn predictive of positive life outcomes (Reicher, 2010).

Turning to teachers, resilience has been investigated by researchers focusing upon identifying risk and protective factors at both individual and contextual levels which are predictive of outcomes such as job satisfaction, stress and teacher retention rates (see Brunetti, 2006). Beltman et al. (2011) carried out a systematic review of fifty studies from ten countries and identified 'personal attributes' (altruism and motivation), self-efficacy, coping skills, interpersonal skills, teaching and instructional skills, and self-reflection to be key protective factors at the individual level. At the contextual level, connectedness and support from school leaders, administrators, mentors, peers and colleagues were identified as key protective factors, together with positive relationships with pupils.

A more recent study by Ainsworth and Oldfield (2019) utilized the statistical technique of relative weight analysis to quantify the relative importance of protective factors at individual and contextual levels. They analysed responses from a questionnaire survey completed by 226 teachers in the UK from thirty-one schools and educational establishments from nursery to sixth form college focusing on predictors of job satisfaction, burnout and teacher well-being. A striking finding from this study was the importance of contextual-level factors. These included 'support from management', 'school culture', 'workload' and 'support from colleagues', and collectively accounted for 55–72 per cent of the variance in scores for well-being, burnout and job satisfaction, respectively. This is in contrast to individual-level protective factors such as 'emotional intelligence', 'perceived conflict' (i.e. between the values of the individual and the expectations of the school), 'self-care' and 'self-esteem'. These individual-level factors collectively accounted for 28–45 per cent of the variance respectively in well-being, burnout and job satisfaction. Further larger scale studies using this analytic approach with longitudinal designs and exploration of possible interactions between protective factors would be helpful, but based upon your experience, how true is it that contextual-level protective factors are more important than individual levels?

Positive psychology and resilience

Finally, resilience is an area of interest for positive psychologists, particularly the study of successful adaption to adversity. 'Positive psychology' (Seligman, 2019; Seligman and Csikszentmihalyi, 2000) was developed in the 1990s in response to the perception of negative bias and overemphasis upon psychopathology. Here, the focus is upon well-being and positive emotions, such as 'hope', 'joy', 'happiness', 'optimism', 'gratitude' and 'forgiveness', and positive character strengths such as 'altruism', 'kindness' and 'creativity'. The impact of systems such as the family, school, workplace and community and the relationships within these are also taken into account (see Arslan, 2019; Kirschman et al., 2009; Luthar et al., 2014).

What can we learn?

Resilience is a complex concept, not a single fixed personality characteristic or trait. The theories and research finding reviewed here suggest that it can be understood in terms of a range of distinctive, active processes involving the interaction of underlying risk and protective factors at the levels of the individual and of the environment. These include the construction of perceptions of the quality of each attachment relationship by IWM (which as we have seen, can impact upon personal and professional relationships across the lifespan) together with appraisal and transactional coping strategies which underpin mechanisms of dealing with stress, either effectively, through the use of problem-focused strategies, or less effectively, via emotion-focused strategies.

Turning to limitations, studies of the effects of heritability upon resilience challenge some of the assumptions of attachment theory, and studies of teacher resilience and transactional coping theory have been criticized for relying upon self-reporting by participants. In addition, some of the assumptions of biosocial models regarding causal influences and the relationship between risk and protective factors have also been criticized (see Ainsworth and Oldfield, 2019; Rutter, 2012).

However, from the theories and research reviewed, the following actions and changes might help teachers to 'thrive' and foster resilience:

- *Develop and maintain a strong professional identity as a teacher*, in terms of commitment, motivation, values and a sense of what it is to be a teacher, as discussed in Chapter 2.
- Make use of *positive coping strategies* focused on embracing and successfully resolving challenges at hand by problem-solving allied to *belief in self* (self-efficacy).
- *Use engagement and connectedness to manage and deal constructively with emotions* (self-regulation) during and following critical incidents through debriefing and sharing with colleagues.
- *Do not take criticism personally*
- *Develop and maintain supportive relationships with colleagues* to provide opportunities for feedback and learning from and through others.
- *Act with integrity and compassion, in line with your beliefs and values* not only in dealings with colleagues but also in pastoral care and relationships with pupils.
- *Develop your interpersonal communication and listening skills*

- *Be aware of policy and practice* and *follow procedures* to make the experience of school culture a positive one.
- *Develop teaching and instructional skills* through awareness of opportunities for professional development.
- *Look after your health and well-being* through adequate sleep, exercise, nutrition and social and personal relationships.

Finally, the study by Riley (2009) in 'Window of research' provides an illustration of the relationship between attachment style and relationships with pupils and the importance of strong professional identity.

Window on research

Riley, P. (2009). 'An adult attachment perspective on the student-teacher relationship and classroom management difficulties', *Teacher and Teaching Education*, 25, pp. 626–35. doi:10.1016/j.tate.2008.11.018

Country: Australia

Age group: Adults (teachers)

Setting: Elementary and secondary schools

Participants Involved: 258 pre-service and 50 experienced elementary and secondary school teachers (66 per cent female; age range 21–59 years [Mean 29.04 years, SD 6.81]).

Aim: The Experience in Close Relationships (ECR) questionnaire was administered to investigate the attachment styles of a sample of teachers to determine whether (a) attachment style had an impact on the decision to choose teaching as a profession as a way of correcting early attachment experiences; (b) experience of teaching (elementary versus secondary) had an impact on attachment style, in regard to the dimensions of anxiety and avoidance; (c) length of experience had an impact on attachment style; and (d) age, gender or being a parent were mediating variables.

Outcomes: The results revealed that the experienced teachers were more secure in their attachments than inexperienced colleagues indicating that some teachers may enter teaching unconsciously in order to correct their early life experiences of attachment and that 'corrective emotional experiences' can be provided in the classroom by the relationships built up by working with pupils, particularly securely attached pupils. In addition, elementary teachers were found to have significantly different attachment styles of teaching over time when compared to secondary colleagues. They were found to be more secure in their relationships than secondary teachers, providing support for the view that the nature of the close day-to-day contact elementary teachers have with their pupils, particularly securely attached pupils, is more likely to provide an emotional experience which can correct early attachment issues. They had lower anxiety levels and formed more close relationships with students. Riley acknowledges that elementary school may provide more opportunities for teachers to develop meaningful relationships given longer periods interacting with the same-class group. Elementary teachers are therefore more likely to get to know their pupils in ways that can foster a deeper emotional connection with them as a function of the time spent together and the variety of activities they engage in. The study revealed that the anxiety levels of experienced teachers were lower where classroom relationships with pupils were positive, which supports the view that relationship building should be part of teacher training. Gender and age were found to be significant mediators and being a parent had no effect, although Riley notes the small sample sizes involved in some of these comparisons.

What we can learn: The adult attachment model helps teachers in two ways. Firstly, by highlighting the needs of both pupils and teachers for positive relationships in the school setting; secondly, by highlighting the importance for teachers of an understanding of attachment theory and of their own attachment style.

Reflective question

How useful are studies of risk and protective factors to an understanding of teacher resilience?

Reflexive question

How might teachers foster resilience by supporting help-seeking by colleagues and pupils?

Understanding reflection

With the demands of planning and organization, curriculum delivery, assessment, monitoring, self-evaluation, reporting, self-evaluation and engagement with pupils, colleagues, parents and other stakeholders alike discussed in Chapter 2, reflection and reflective practice may be regarded as central to the work of a teacher.

Dewey (1933, p. 118) defined reflection as 'active, persistent, and careful consideration of any belief or supposed form of knowledge in the light of the grounds that support it and the further conclusions to which it tends'. Rogers (2002) notes the complexity and breadth of the concept is borne out by the thirty or so terms that he used in his book to characterize it! While acknowledging that the term 'reflection' per se has wider scope if we consider its relevance to all aspects of life (Fook, 2007; Rogers, 2002), we will focus on 'reflection' in regard to the professional practice and education of teachers. That is, on the 'reflective practice' which can achieve change in schools and classrooms as a result of the awareness and understandings that can be constructed and drawn from experiential learning.

Examples of 'theories' of reflection and reflective practice

Larrivee (2008) identifies four developmental 'levels' of reflection, contrasting the more descriptive reflections of inexperienced teachers ('pre-reflection' and 'surface reflection') with the levels of reflection which link theory to practice and take pupil and student outcomes into account which are more characteristic of experienced teachers ('pedagogical reflection' and 'critical reflection'). But how does experience impact upon depth of reflection? To understand this, we turn to David Kolb's (1984) four-stage 'cycle of learning'.

Kolb's model explains the underlying learning process involved in terms of Piagetian theory, specifically the process of the incorporation of new information in 'schemas' by the processes of assimilation and accommodation. The cycle of 'concrete experience', followed by 'reflective observation', then 'abstract conceptualization' and finally 'active experimentation' describes how we learn from experience through transformative processes of reflecting, developing new concepts or ideas or modifying existing ones, and then acting upon these new insights by implementing what has been learned in practice. Kolb's theory further holds that individuals have preferred learning 'styles' and tend to emphasize one of the four dimensions more than the others.

In contrast, as we saw in Chapter 1, Schön (1983) distinguishes two types of reflection. *Reflection-in-action* refers to 'thinking while doing', the analysis, evaluation and re-framing of problems, taking context and situations into account and improvising possible responses 'in the moment', what Schön (1987) refers to as 'professional artistry' of teaching. It is possible to further reflect upon reflection-in-action, a process that Schön refers to as *reflection-on-action*, making sense of and learning from the experience, which may have an indirect effect upon future action. Eraut (1995, p. 16) argues that the distinction between these two types of reflection may not be as clear-cut as Schön suggests, and proposes a third type of reflection,

reflection-for-action, which he holds is more explicitly linked to the development and improvement of future practice.

Brookfield (1998, p. 197) has written about the importance of 'critical reflection' and 'critically reflective practice', which he defines as 'a process of inquiry involving practitioners in trying to discover, and research, the assumptions that frame how they work'. This process of 'research' entails viewing professional practice critically through four distinct but complementary 'lenses': an *autobiographical lens*, that is, a teacher's lens as a learner which in turn helps reflection on their performance as a teacher; the *lens of the learner*, that is, taking the learner's perspective into account reflecting on the implications for teaching; the *lens of the experience of colleagues*, that is, taking into account professional peers' views and perceptions of problems and underlying assumptions; and the *lens of the theoretical literature*, helping the teacher to take into account relevant theories, research and other evidence, again to reflect upon assumptions.

These 'lenses' highlight the 'power dynamics' – explicit and implicit – in all work settings, of which the practitioner has to be aware. The theory is grounded in critical theory which informs understandings of the need for awareness of 'hegemonic assumptions', that is, 'assumptions that we think are in our own best interests that actually work against us in the long term' (Brookfield, 1998, p. 197).

Finally, Rolfe et al. (2001) developed a model of 'triad reflection' which requires teachers to consider and reflect upon three questions: What? So what? Now what? There are parallels between this model and that of Kolb as triad reflection requires the teacher to consider a situation and what happened there; then to make sense of the meaning of this experience; and lastly, to reflect upon what to do to move things on.

Reflective question
How do these theories help you to understand your own process of reflection as a teacher?

... and reflexivity

'Reflexivity' has its origins in the ways in which social constructionist theorists sought to account for the impact on the interpretation of research findings of the positionality, perspective, values (both personal as well as 'espoused' such as those of organization) and the 'personal epistemology' (beliefs about the nature of knowledge and evidence) of the investigator (Bourdieu, 2004; Burr, 2003; Feucht et al., 2017; Giddens, 1991; Hibbert et al., 2010). More recently, the term has been extended to professional practice of teachers (Feucht et al., 2017; Fook, 2007; Ryan and Bourke, 2013).

As Bolton (2010) notes, 'to be reflexive' in professional practice is to consider the impact upon inclusion and equity of institutional structures, power dynamics and knowledge and awareness. This entails a questioning of attitudes, values and beliefs in regard to professional roles and engagement with others. Building upon the work of Archer (2012), Feucht and colleagues (2017, p. 234) further characterize the process of reflexivity in the context of teaching as 'an internal dialogue that leads to action for transformative practices in the classroom'. Questioning understandings by means of internal dialogue in this way is the underlying mechanism by which reflection becomes reflexivity. Evidence from case studies suggests that reflexivity is associated with transformative and sustainable change in teaching and instruction in educational settings (Feucht et al., 2017; Hibbert et al., 2010; Ryan and Bourke, 2013). Further, as Hibbert and colleagues (2010) point out, through this questioning process, reflexivity in turn impacts upon reflection, thus defining a recursive relationship between the two processes.

Hibbert and colleagues provide a conceptual framework consisting of four 'modes' of reflexivity (repetition, extension, disruption and participation) with transition between modes underpinned by processes of internal dialogues (Hibbert et al., 2010, pp. 51–8) although they do not provide any empirical support for their model.

Winkler (2014) provides a view from her professional experience as a social worker with looked-after children which links reflexivity, resilience and attachment. Here, the foundations of 'reflexivity' lie in securely attached relationships in the early years which are in turn associated with the development of processes of self-regulation in the brain which underpin reflexivity and resilience (see Fonagy and Target, 2002). She argues that resilient individuals able to adapt to adverse experiences do so because of their ability to make sense of what has happened to them and holds that reflexivity is 'the hallmark of resilience' (Winkler, 2014, p. 470). Or as Kraemer (1999, pp. 6–7) puts it, 'The resilient individual is the one who can understand what has happened to them.'

Reflexive practice has an important role in the development of teacher professional identity (Stîngu, 2012), with studies of teachers' blogs revealing the growth of reflexivity as pre-service teachers become more experienced (see Garza and Smith, 2015). Some researchers highlight the importance of experience-based, reflexive teaching in schools to encourage both critique of values and assumptions and purposive action (Duarte and Fitzgerald, 2006).

What can we learn?

Theory and research highlight the importance both of experience and experiential learning and of the perspectives of learners, colleagues and other stakeholders. The questioning of knowledge and of understandings through internal dialogue for the transition from reflection to reflexivity is key, with evidence from case studies indicating that this transition may facilitate transformative change in the classroom.

Systematic reviews such as that of Beltman and colleagues (2011) provide evidence for a relationship between reflection and teachers' job satisfaction and well-being, although there are fewer studies of the relationship between reflective and reflexive teaching practice and pupil and student adjustment, achievement and outcomes.

As we noted in Chapter 2, a systematic review by Zee and Koomen (2016) revealed positive associations between measures of the teachers' self-efficacy and their psychological well-being based upon 165 studies carried out over a forty-year period. While the findings regarding teacher self-efficacy and pupil achievement were less clear-cut, there were associations between teacher self-efficacy and the quality of classroom practices and the pupils' academic adjustment. In a more recent prospective study carried out in the United States, Summers and colleagues (2017) in a more recent study found that teachers' self-efficacy beliefs were predictive of the quality of perceptions of teacher–pupil relationships, with more confident teachers with higher expectations tending to have less conflict and better relationships with their 11–13-year-old pupils.

However, turning to student achievement, in a large-scale prospective longitudinal study of 300 teachers in England over three academic sessions, Sammons et al. (2007) found that such dimensions of teacher professional identity as commitment, motivation and resilience accounted for 15–30 per cent in pupil academic outcomes in pupils aged between 12 and 16 years. Finally, a recent small-scale study by Akbari and colleagues (2008) reported a significant relationship between the scores of thirty Iranian teachers on a scale of reflective practice and their high school pupils' performance on an end-of-year assessment ($p < .018$). Although there are caveats regarding the size of sample, the use of self-reporting, and the cross-sectional design which limits conclusions regarding possible causal links, this study is of interest as it indicates a link between teachers' self-reflection and pupils' achievement while also accounting for the effects of the teachers' self-efficacy.

Conclusion

In this chapter, we considered the case for considering 'resilience', 'reflection' and 'reflexivity' as a new 'Three Rs'. We reviewed relevant theories and research and key understandings concluding that 'resilience' may best be regarded as a dynamic process involving the interaction of factors at individual and contextual levels which can account for outcomes such as teacher's job satisfaction and well-being. Research findings which stress the importance of attachment history were also considered.

We noted that reflection and reflexivity are integral to the role of the teacher and underpin self-evaluation, planning at both individual and collaborative levels, and links between theory and practice in effective teaching. The importance of 'thinking while doing', of making sense of experiential learning, of taking on board the perspectives of others, and of intentional internal dialogues were also noted. However, the need for further research including pupil outcomes was also discussed.

But can we relate reflection, reflexivity and resilience? The case study illustrates a coherent and 'joined up' approach to conceptualizing the 'Three Rs' of resilience, reflection and reflexivity by exploring the contribution of these three concepts to an understanding of classroom management style.

Case study: Can attachment theory, reflection and reflexivity inform teacher classroom behaviour management style?

Country: UK

Age group: Pupils in Year 3 (aged between 6 and 7 years)

Setting: Mainstream primary/elementary school

Participants involved: Experienced class teacher, trusted colleagues, head teacher and educational psychologist

Case study: Carol is a primary teacher with 4 years of teaching experience who shared concerns with her Head-teacher about the attention-seeking behaviour of a Year 3 (7 years old) pupil who had recently been removed from the care of his parents as a result of their ongoing drug misuse.

The Head-teacher suggested a consultation with the educational psychologist working with the school on developing attachment-informed practice. The educational psychologist met with Carol and they scheduled two coaching and mentoring sessions and a follow-up.

The first session explored the impact of the boy's early life experiences on his attachment and Carol reflected on her own attachment history as a child. Carol's mother had mental health difficulties and was dependent on Carol. Roles became reversed and Carol began to resent her mother's vulnerability and need for attention. Carol used practical problem-solving questions such as: 'What happened and why?' 'What can I do differently next time?' to reflect on her strong feelings about the pupil. This provided the insight that her feelings of irritation towards the pupil were linked to her own childhood attachment relationship with her mother. To explore this further, Carol engaged in reflexivity, standing back from her usual ways of thinking and using internal dialogue to further examine her preconceptions about the situation and their impact on her relationship with the pupil and how the pupil might be perceiving her. To do this, she used reflexive questions such as: 'How do I influence the pupil's behaviour?' 'How do my values, beliefs, experiences and expectations influence how I interpret the pupil's behaviour?' 'How do my values, beliefs, experiences and expectations influence my response to this behaviour?' 'How do I now view my own attachment history?' 'Do I need to change my ideas and behaviour in the light of this?' She then shared with two trustworthy colleagues her new understandings that the pupil's attention-seeking was related to his insecure attachment history and that her own attachment history was impacting upon her interpretation of the pupil's behaviour, her response, and her relationship with her pupil, all of which was likely to make the pupil more anxious.

During the second session with the psychologist, Carol reported that she was less reactive and irritated by the pupil but was still trying to identify an effective intervention. Carol proposed a non-intrusive approach to reassure the pupil that he was being 'kept in mind', an example of reflexivity effecting transformative change in teaching practice. The strategy entailed the use of an agreed and unobtrusive signal to reassure the pupil that he was not forgotten, and that Carol would attend to his needs when she had time to do so.

Back in class, Carol asked the pupil for a small drawing to attach to the back of her ID badge. She explained to him that she understood how hard it was to wait for the teacher when you have something important to ask. She told the pupil that when it was not possible for her to respond right away that she would turn her ID badge to show his drawing to let him know that she had not forgotten him and that she would respond as soon as she could.

Feedback to the educational psychologist three weeks later in the follow-up session confirmed that the concrete reassurance of the drawing was working and that the pupil was self-regulating his own behaviour and was less attention-seeking.

Outcomes: Through reflection and reflexivity, Carol became aware of why a pupil might constantly seek the teacher's attention. She became confident in establishing appropriate classroom strategies and realized how her own attachment history had affected her emotional response to the pupil.

What we can learn: Attachment theory is relevant to the dynamics of the classroom and can inform strategies for dealing with challenging behaviour. As Carol demonstrated, reflection and reflexivity focused on one's own attachment history provides insight into emotional responses towards pupils and how these can colour the interpretation of pupils' behaviour. However, awareness of this can lead to a more effective classroom management style.

> **Reflective questions**
>
> 1. How important is 'experiential learning' for professional development?
> 2. How important is an awareness of power dynamics for you as a teacher?

> **Reflexive questions**
>
> 1. What contribution has self-awareness of your professional practice made to change in your classroom or school?
> 2. In what ways have you used internal dialogue to question your attitudes, values and beliefs in regard to professional roles and engagement with others?

Implications for teachers

- Teachers should be aware that children and young people who have experienced difficulties in their relationships with their parents or carers may present specific challenges within the classroom in terms of the expression of emotion and regulation of behaviour and in their response to learning tasks.
- It is important for teachers to reflect on their own IWM and attachment style to help to promote secure and positive relationships with their pupils.
- Schools should have robust procedures for identifying concerns, assessing need and risk, and preparing plans of action to support vulnerable pupils. These will include individuals who have been removed from the care of their birth parents and are fostered or adopted as well as all other children where adverse life experiences might threaten or challenge healthy development.
- Experiential learning which takes into account the perspectives of pupils, colleagues and other stakeholders facilitates the development of reflective practice.
- Questioning of values, beliefs and understandings through purposive internal dialogue facilitates the transition from reflection to reflexivity.
- Transformative change in the classroom is underpinned by reflexive practice.

Annotated bibliography

Reicher, H. (2010). 'Building inclusive education on social and emotional learning: Challenges and perspectives – a review', *International Journal of Inclusive Education,* **14(3), pp. 213–46. doi:10.1080/13603110802504218.**
A thoughtful account of theory and research regarding risk, protective factors and resilience highlighting links between adaptive systems moderating and mediating the effects of resilience.

Fook, J. (2007). 'Reflective practice and critical reflection', in Lishman, J. (ed.) *Handbook for practice learning in social work and social care, second edition: Knowledge and theory.* **London: Jessica Kingsley.**
A theoretical overview and critique of reflection and reflexivity linked to professional practice.

7
Psychology and the Effective Teacher

Lisa Marks Woolfson, James Boyle and Jeremy Monsen

This volume has been underpinned by the overarching assumption that teachers can develop their competence and confidence by utilizing their experiences in a reflective manner. Furthermore, operating as a reflective practitioner to improve practice is a process that we, the editors, view as continuing throughout a teacher's career. Our aim in these chapters therefore has been to support teachers through this ongoing formative learning process to help them understand the different facets and complexities of their role, and to enable them to communicate with their colleagues, students and parents/carers, with insight, confidence and critical understanding. Another of our key assumptions was that the inherent challenges in doing this are simply part of the job, so we wanted to help teachers realize what barriers they could expect in this role, and to offer some insights and practical strategies.

The chapters in this book suggest several different ways that these important tasks can be achieved by utilizing theory and evidence-led understandings from the field of psychology.

The book offers psychological frameworks and tools to enable teachers' critical reflection with the intention of leading to improved and more effective ways of thinking and acting in the classroom. The coaching model in Chapter 1 and the Accessible Dialogue framework in Chapter 5 are helpful examples of psychological approaches to how teachers can manage real-world dilemmas in practice through active reflection on one's thinking and actions.

We have drawn not only on theories and reported research findings from educational, developmental, social and cognitive psychology, but also from health psychology and work psychology. Findings discussed here extend across the range of research designs and methodologies used by psychologists. These include questionnaire surveys and interviews, case studies, observational studies, longitudinal and follow-up studies, experimental/quasi-experimental studies and systematic reviews. They include quantitative data analysis, the analysis of numerical data, and qualitative data analysis, non-numerical data such as transcripts of interviews. We hope this reporting of research studies aids understanding of the role and value of psychology for teachers and indeed that it will be particularly useful to readers who are going on to carry out their own research projects in the classroom, when adopting the scientist-practitioner role, as explained in Chapter 1. We, the three editors of this volume, all psychologists and trained teachers, view psychology as having a central place for teachers developing their 'craft' and practitioner stance, and that it has had a positive influence over educational thinking and practice since its inception over 200 years ago when it broke away from the disciplines of philosophy, physiology and physics.

Some background on psychology in education

When and how did psychology apply itself to education? It is generally agreed that psychology itself became a distinct academic discipline in 1879 when Wilhelm Wundt opened the first experimental psychology laboratory at the University of Leipzig. Psychology was certainly being taught in other universities at that time, for example, William James at Harvard University and John Dewey at the University of Chicago. It was not however taught as a separate discipline or taught by professors who were specifically psychologists. James's background, for example, was medicine and Dewey was an educator and philosopher. Students from many countries, especially the United States, came to study psychology at Wundt's laboratory, and then went back home and set up their own departments. In this way, the new discipline of psychology spread. It had grown out of philosophy, physiology and physics and was initially focused on measurement of mental and perceptual processes. But how did we get from measuring reaction times, which was a favourite scientific method of assessing psychological processes in Wundt's lab, to applying psychology to education?

William James was certainly one of the first to have an interest in extending the focus of interest of this new field of psychology to the problems of education. He gave lectures to teachers about applying psychology to teaching and then published the talks in his book *Talks to teachers and to students on some of life's ideals* in 1899. This book was regularly reprinted, demonstrating its popularity and its relevance to the theory of education.

At around the same time, John Dewey was undertaking cutting-edge work at the University of Chicago, founding the Laboratory School there. This was a pioneer experimental school that began with one teacher and twelve pupils for the purpose of allowing Dewey to try out new teaching methods to change the curriculum. He was one of the first to utilize a one-way mirror system so he could see what was happening in semi-naturalistic settings like the classroom, without the participants being aware. In this way Dewey was able to apply and test his progressive ideas around how teachers teach and how pupils learn. This became known as the progressive education movement.

Although Wundt is usually viewed as the 'father of psychology', it is Edward Thorndike who is seen as the founder of educational psychology specifically. Thorndike was a student of William James who wanted to extend the application of psychology to understand how children learn – the beginning of psychology's interest in learning and the beginnings of educational psychology. Thorndike studied learning behaviour in animals as well as in children. A famous study involved cats in a puzzle box where the cats learned to pull a lever to get themselves out of the box.

Thorndike published a book in 1906 on principles of teaching based upon psychology. His law of effect emphasized that behaviour and learning were a result of experiences rather than the result of instinct. This way of thinking put the onus firmly in the hands of teachers then to organize and structure classroom experiences that would result in learning. This was in contrast to it being viewed rather as the children's task to gather knowledge and information for themselves. Thorndike was highly prolific in carrying out his research and published widely. The application of psychology to educational practice was now under way.

At around this time in France, primary education had become compulsory, but it was recognized that regular education was not suitable for all children and that some children would require special education. But which children? To solve this problem, Alfred Binet became interested in the measurement of the cognitive abilities, 'intelligence', of children. He recognized that a psychology discipline focused upon experimental laboratory studies of perception and response times was not suitable for the task in hand. The problem was that these measurements did not distinguish between children of different levels of 'intelligence'. Working with a medical student, Theodore Simon, Binet developed a standardized questionnaire and tasks that typically developing children of different ages could be expected to succeed on. In 1907 this work resulted in the first validated intelligence test with norms reflecting the items that children of different ages could be expected to succeed at. In the twentieth century cognitive psychologists such as George Miller and Ulric Neisser were interested in studying memory and the processing of information in adults. Jean Piaget, a Swiss psychologist, studied cognitive development, how children develop important concepts and understandings through different ages and stages.

Over the course of the twentieth century, the principles of educational psychology became embedded in teacher education as well as in classroom practice and education policy. Teachers began to study educational and child psychology in their training as its influence on how best to provide learning experiences for children in the classroom was now recognized. Educational psychology provides theories and research findings that provide an understanding of the relevant processes which underlie the cognitive, social, emotional and behavioural functioning of pupils in the social contexts of schools and classrooms. You will have come across in your training, and since, the work of eminent educationalists and psychologists such as Maria Montessori, Benjamin Bloom and Robert Gagné in the application of psychology to the practice of teaching; B.F. Skinner and Albert Bandura to theories of learning; and Jean Piaget, Lev Vygotsky and Jerome Bruner to theories of social, moral and cognitive development in children.

The application of psychology to children's classroom experience is now a well-established part of the teachers' professional toolkit. But we three editors decided we wanted to go beyond the application of psychology as it is applied to teaching and learning. We recognized that teachers also need to know about, not only that psychology which can be applied to the children they teach, but also psychology that they can apply to themselves. We wanted to introduce to you the psychology that teachers need to help in the challenge of their role. Consequently, in this volume, we considered key themes identified by theories and research from the wider range of psychologies which impact upon the experience of being a teacher.

Reflection and reflexivity

Reflection was considered in Chapters 1 and 2 in regard to planning and self-evaluation and again in more detail in Chapter 6 together with reflexivity. Different theories were considered to help you recognize cycles of reflection as well as different developmental levels of reflection, ranging from descriptive reflection of new teachers to the more critical stance of experienced teachers, linking theory and practice. You learned in Chapter 6 to distinguish between reflection-in-action and reflection-for-action, of 'thinking while doing', which emphasizes the importance of experiential learning and of the need to consider the perspectives of others. The importance of internal dialogue as the mechanism whereby reflection becomes reflexivity was also discussed, together with case studies indicating a recursive relationship between reflection and reflexivity and links with change which is both transformative and sustainable. The importance of experiential learning together with the use of purposive internal dialogue to question values, beliefs and understandings and hence to support the transition from reflection to reflexivity was also considered.

Chapter 1 moreover highlighted the significance of quality feedback from a 'critical friend' to guide the reflective process for the development of teacher self-efficacy. The contribution of the coaching model with a peer, a parent/carer or a more experienced practitioner to aid this reflection was examined. The importance of self-efficacy was discussed in Chapter 3. It is a key determinant of effective teaching, of job satisfaction and commitment, distinguishing between those who leave the profession and those who stay. Furthermore, self-efficacy is related to resilience which is introduced in Chapter 3 and discussed in greater depth in Chapter 6.

Professional identity

Both Chapters 2 and 3 addressed teacher professional identity and the importance of context and expectations with respect to the roles and responsibilities of a teacher. Chapter 2's thematic analysis of the sample of job descriptions helped to crystallize the 'what' of teaching and the associated expectations of an effective teacher. It emphasized the importance of context, particularly of the social world of the classroom, school and the influences of society. Chapter 3's focus was particularly on the developing role identity of beginning teachers as they become part of the professional group of teachers. Issues around social identity and belonging to groups are important for you to understand because of issues of agency, how the group that you see yourself belonging to, can influence our actions and behaviours. This chapter discussed the psychology of groups using social identity theory and explored the management of potential role ambiguities and conflicts and considered how to ensure professional boundaries are retained. Both Chapters 2 and 3 examined in complementary ways how a teacher's sense of professional identity is shaped by roles, responsibilities and relationships in the social world of schools and classrooms.

As well as social identity theory, insights from identity theory and 'figured worlds' theory supported a view of teacher professional identity as socially constructed through narratives and discourse and experience of teaching in the social world of schools. These chapters further highlighted the importance of personal history, beliefs and values in shaping professional identity over the course of a teaching career. They indicated the importance of teachers' understanding of child and adolescent cognitive, social, psychosexual and emotional development together with awareness of trans and LGBTQ issues for the effective delivery of teaching, and pastoral roles in particular.

Well-being

Chapter 3 focused on psychological, personal, social and emotional aspects of teacher well-being. Psychological perspectives on autonomy, resilience and avoiding stress and burnout in the classroom were also explored in this chapter. It acknowledged that there is a worryingly high dropout rate for teachers in their first few years in the job and recognized that it is necessary for teachers to engage in strategies to enhance their mental health and avoid stress and burnout in the complex setting of the school. You will have learned here that well-being can be about a hedonic perspective. That is to say, enjoying your job, where you experience job satisfaction, and you feel on balance more positive than negative emotions in your daily work. But well-being can encompass an eudaimonic perspective with a focus on more psychological dimensions. For this, the job provides opportunities for personal growth and fulfilment, a sense of purpose, or a context for the mastery of new skills, or achievement of professional goals. In Chapter 3 different ways of measuring well-being in the workplace were also discussed, including antecedent factors that contribute to well-being at work and outcomes of interventions intended to improve well-being.

An important aspect of this is autonomy, the extent to which teachers feel they have personal control in the workplace, to what degree they feel they have independence in the classroom. We recognized that teachers may feel they have limited control over the timing of their working hours and their daily schedule within those hours, but they may however feel some degree of control over the classroom activities they choose to deliver to promote prescribed learning and curricular objectives. This is likely to differ markedly across countries, local boards and across individual schools. It may be useful to reflect on what the balance is for you personally in your current role, and how you feel about that as we know that autonomy is associated with motivation, job satisfaction and stress and burnout, and that these are all critical factors in the world of work.

Social relationships

The point was made in Chapter 3 of the importance of building networks so that you have a community to support you in the challenges you face as a teacher. These networks can comprise colleagues, friends and family, peers, mentors and supervisors. Different relationships can provide encouragement and advice at different times and for different issues.

But of course, social relationships apply within the classroom itself and Chapter 4 examined social contextual issues in the class setting, focusing on teacher–pupil relationships and interactions, as well as peer interactions. We examined what psychology has to say about the best ways to group pupils in the classroom and the extent to which ability groups were effective for educational outcomes, for behavioural outcomes and for social outcomes. The authors reported studies that found a relationship between ability grouping and grouping across socioeconomic and ethnic lines, drawing our attention to the issue that ability grouping can indeed further exacerbate groupings that already exist in society. Chapter 5 examined the social world of the classroom in regard to the nature of the classroom environment and the effects of its physical organization and available resources upon pupils' interactions with the teacher and their peers, together with the roles of cooperative and collaborative group work. How you can use insights from humanistic psychology to help you to be more genuine in these pupil–teacher interactions was discussed in Chapter 3.

Attachment theory research considered in Chapter 6 further highlighted the importance of relationships in the developing child. Studies indicate that it is important for teachers to be aware of the impact of pupil's adverse experiences and difficulties in their relationships with parents/carers on self-regulation of their emotions and behaviour. Current research in Chapter 6 introduced the more recent application of attachment theory beyond the relationships between parent/carers and children to teacher–pupil relationships. Further, as teacher's own attachment history may have an impact upon their expectations of, and relationships with their pupils, awareness of this is important for the teacher in the interest of developing secure, positive relationships in the classroom.

Communication

When we consider the many interactions that a new teacher takes part in in the course of a day, the importance of effective communication for joint problem-solving cannot be overemphasized. Communication was a pervasive theme throughout this volume – communicating with pupils, with colleagues, with parents/carers and with line managers. Chapter 5 explored that we all often make faulty assumptions and attributions about others' intentions when we communicate with them and discussed how this can lead to problems. In this chapter we viewed communication as a core skill to be mastered and to aid this we presented Accessible Dialogue, a framework to guide teachers towards improved communication with a focus on joint problem-solving. We wanted to help teachers raise difficult issues in ways that have the potential for positive outcomes. To do this we recommended that teachers use this, or a similar framework to clarify the thinking that underpins their verbal behaviour. This means that in a professional interaction you would make explicit what you are thinking and why you are thinking this. Important concepts here are 'espoused theory' and 'theory-in-use'. You want to search for inconsistencies by analysing valid information. This allows any previously hidden agenda to be discussed openly and your views to be tested out. This is all a means to communicating more effectively with colleagues in order to generate better solutions to problems that have presented. The next suggested step for acquiring these skills is role-play with supervisor support.

In the present day, much communication takes place through social media, Facebook, Twitter, email, blogs. Technology can aid timely communication between teachers, professional networks, parents/carers and pupils as well as be a valuable teaching tool. Online homework planners, online assignments, newsletters, access to internet resources, email contact between school and home, are good examples of effective use of technology in education. Parents and carers are often members of class WhatsApp groups which allow information about their child's class to be shared between them, although as with all closed groups there is a danger that these can operate as an echo chamber sharing misinformation that the teacher then has to address. In your professional role as a teacher, you may compose and send an email intended only for an individual pupil or parent/carer but bear in mind that the recipient can choose to share its contents with the wider school community. Teachers should therefore view electronic messages to pupils or parents/carers as potentially available to a wider public and existing forever. Ensure that you are familiar with policies for social media communication in your school and school district and be very clear of the boundaries between the private and the professional.

Resilience

The importance of resilience for teacher well-being is another key theme of this volume and was considered in Chapters 3 and 6. The concept was discussed in Chapter 6 as one of the 'new 3Rs', with reference to understandings drawn from attachment theory, transactional coping theory, biosocial models such diathesis-stress model; developmental tasks, and positive psychology, together with research studies of the interplay between risk and protective factors. A key question posed in this chapter was, 'is resilience a competence that can be developed, or is it a character strength, an aspect of personality, a core-, or domain-specific, capacity?' The findings from research studies indicate that resilience is best conceptualized as a dynamic process involving factors at both individual and contextual levels. Individual protective factors include motivation, self-efficacy, interpersonal skills, instructional skills, coping skills and self-reflection. Contextual factors relate to support from colleagues, managers and mentors, and positive relationships with pupils and students. Resilience is associated with a range of important outcomes such as teacher mental health and job satisfaction.

Conclusions and next steps

1. Construct for yourself a strong, well-thought-out teacher professional identity. At regular intervals, remind yourself why you decided to become a teacher and what you value in teaching. Aim to keep in touch with these values, so you are clear about your purpose and the importance of the job you do.
2. Build yourself social networks for mentoring, collaboration and support to facilitate your ongoing personal and professional development.
3. Keep a constant eye on and actively monitor your work–life balance.

4. Continue to develop your pedagogical knowledge, subject expertise and classroom skills to build teacher self-efficacy. Make good use of professional development opportunities.
5. While subject knowledge, instructional skills and well-planned delivery of the curriculum are central to effective teaching, understand that learning is more than the transmission of knowledge from teacher to pupil. In addition, think about how to develop the social context of the classroom and foster social relationships through which children learn from each other, and form attitudes and beliefs as they grow up.
6. Have high expectations for all the pupils in your classroom.
7. Think about how you might develop your interpersonal and listening skills to ensure you can communicate effectively with pupils, colleagues, parents and line managers.
8. Challenging interactions and difficult situations will occur from time to time in your work as a teacher. Be prepared by developing and practising a way of dealing with these that lead to positive problem-solving. We have suggested the Accessible Dialogue framework in this volume as an example that is applicable for use in the school setting.
9. Take care of your health and well-being. Think about diet, exercise, sleep, personal relationships, and how to manage and reduce stress. This will all help to build your resilience in the workplace.
10. Learn from your mistakes but draw a line and move on from them and instead make the main focus of your attention where a lesson, dealing with a challenging pupil, or a tricky meeting with a parent/carer, went well. You might even like to note these good examples down for future reference – it's easy to forget these with all that happens day to day.

And finally ...

New teachers will often say that they just want to 'get through' their first year of teaching. They know this first year will be challenging, intellectually, emotionally and physically. A key aim of this volume was to show how psychology can help teachers not just survive, but rather thrive, grow and then to continue to develop professionally as effective practitioners, with a high level of job satisfaction.

Our philosophy is that psychology can be a force for good in the life of the teacher. We hope that this book will serve as a starting point for your next steps of finding out more about the application of psychology to education and thinking how to take account of it in your day-to-day activities. We are sure that this will enrich your experience as a teacher and your pupils' experience as learners in your classroom.

References

Chapter 1 Setting the Context
Jeremy Monsen, Lisa Marks Woolfson, and James Boyle

Arygris, C. and Schön, D. A. (1974). *Theory into practice*. San Francisco, CA: Jossey-Bass.

Arygris, C. and Schön, D. A. (1996). *Organisational learning II: Theory, method and practice*. Reading, MA: Addison Wesley.

Baines, E., Blatchford, P. and Kutnick, P. (2016). *Promoting effective group work in the primary classroom: A handbook for teachers and practitioners*. 2nd edn. London: Routledge.

Bullough, R., Young, J., Erickson, L., Birrell, J., Clark, D., Egan, M., Berrie, C., Hales, V. and Smith, G. (2002). 'Rethinking field experience: Partnership teaching versus single-placement teaching', *Journal of Teacher Education*, 53(1), pp. 68–80.

Cameron, R. J. and Monsen, J. J. (1998). 'Coaching and critical dialogue in educational psychology practice', *Educational and Child Psychology*, 15(4), pp. 112–26.

Cevik, Y. D., Haşlaman, T. and Çelik, S. (2015). 'The effect of peer assessment on problem solving skills of prospective teachers supported by online learning activities', *Studies in Educational Evaluation*, 44, pp. 23–35.

Chizhik, E. W., Chizhik, A. W., Close, C. and Gallego, M. (2018). 'Developing student teachers' teaching self-efficacy through Shared Mentoring in Learning Environments (SMILE)', *International Journal of Mentoring and Coaching in Education*, 7(1), pp. 35–53.

Darling-Hammond, L. (2006). *Powerful teacher education: Lessons from exemplary programs*. San Francisco, CA: Wiley.

Dewey, J. (1929). *The sources of a science of education*. The Kappa Delta Pi Lecture Series. New York: Horace Liveright.

Dewey, J. (1933). *How we think: A restatement of the relation of reflective thinking to the educative process*. Boston, MA: D. C. Heath and Co. (Originally published in 1910).

Dryden, W. (2019). *Helping clients deal with adversity by changing their attitudes: A concise therapists guide*. Abingdon, OX: Routledge.

Egan, G. (2014). *The skilled helper*. 10th edn. Belmont, CA: Brooks/Cole, Cengage Learning.

Fullan, M. (2010). *All systems go: The change imperative for whole system reform. Motion leadership: The skinny on becoming change savvy*. Thousand Oaks, CA: Corwin/Sage.

Glenn, W. J. (2006). 'Model versus mentor: Defining the necessary qualities of the effective cooperating teacher', *Teacher Education Quarterly*, 33(1), pp. 85–95.

Hattie, J. (2009). *Visible learning: A synthesis of over 800 meta-analyses relating to achievement*. Milton Park, UK: Routledge.

Hattie, J. (2012). *Visible learning for teachers: Maximising impact on learning*. Milton Park, UK: Routledge.

Hobson, A. J. (2016). 'Judge mentoring and how to avert it: Introducing ONSIDE Mentoring for beginning teachers', *International Journal of Mentoring and Coaching in Education*, 5(2), pp. 87–110.

Inhelder, B. and Piaget, J. (1958). *The growth of logical thinking from childhood to adolescence*. New York: Basic Books.

Kearney, D. (1994). *Coaching*. Yeovil, Somerset: Organisational and Personal Development Consultants.

Kelly, B. and Perkins, D. (eds.) (2012). *The Cambridge handbook of implementation science for educational psychology*. Cambridge: Cambridge University Press, pp. 132–49.

Kennedy, E. and Monsen, J. J. (2016). 'Evidence based practice in educational and child psychology: Opportunities for practitioner-researchers using problem-based methodology', *Educational and Child Psychology*, 33(3), pp. 11–25.

Korthagen, F. (2004). 'In search of the essence of a good teacher: Towards a more holistic approach in teacher education', *Teaching and Teacher Education*, 20(1), pp. 77–97.

Korthagen, F. (2010). 'Situated learning theory and the pedagogy of teacher education: Towards an integrative view of teacher behavior and teacher learning', *Teaching and Teacher Education*, 26, pp. 98–106.

Lyle, J. (2002). *Sports coaching concepts: A framework for coaches' behaviours*. Abingdon, OX: Routledge.

Lyle, J. and Cushion, C. (2017). *Sport coaching concepts: A framework for coaching practice*. Abingdon, OX: Routledge.

Lynch, D. (2014). 'Improving teaching through coaching, mentoring and feedback: A review of literature', *MIER Journal of Educational Studies, Trends and Practices*, 4(2), pp. 136–66.

Monsen, J. J. and Cameron, R. J. (2002). 'Supporting and developing teachers' practice through coaching', in P. Gray (ed.) *Working with emotions: Responding to the challenges of difficult pupil behaviour in schools*. London: Routledge, pp. 151–68.

Monsen, J. J. and Woolfson, L. (2012). 'The role of executive problem solving frameworks in preparing for effective change in educational contexts', in Kelly, B. and Perkins, D. (eds.) *The Cambridge handbook of implementation science for educational psychology*. Cambridge: Cambridge University Press, pp. 132–49.

Nelson-Jones, R. (2014). *Nelson-Jones' theory and practice of counselling and psychotherapy*. 6th edn. London: Sage.

Perry, R. R. and Lewis, C.C. (2009). 'What is successful adaptation of lesson study in the US?' *Journal of Educational Change*, 10, pp. 365–91.

Pound, L. (2006). *How children learn*. London, UK: Practical Pre-school Books, MA Education Ltd.

Robinson, V. (1993). *Problem based methodology: Research for the improvement of practice*. Oxford: Pergamon.

Robinson, V. (2018). *Reduce change to increase improvement*. Corwin, CA: Sage.

Sato, M. and Loewen, S. (2018). 'Do teachers care about research? The research–pedagogy dialogue', *ELT Journal*, 73(1), pp. 1–10.

Schön, D. A. (1983). *The reflective practitioner – How professionals think in action*. New York/USA: Basic Book.

Schön, D. A. (1987). *Educating the reflective practitioner*. San Francisco, CA: Jossey-Bass.

Shoffner, M., Brown, M., Platt, B., Long, M. and Salyer, B. (2010). 'Meeting the challenge: Beginning English teachers reflect on their first year', *English Journal*, 99(6), pp. 70–7.

Smith, R. and Lynch, D. (2014). 'Coaching and mentoring: A review of literature as it relates to teacher professional development', *International Journal of Innovation, Creativity and Change*, 1(4), pp. 91–103.

Stahl, G., Sharplin, E. and Kehrwald, B. (2016). 'Developing pre-service teachers' confidence: Real-time coaching in teacher education', *Reflective Practice*, 17(6), pp. 724–38.

Vikaraman, S. S., Mansor, A. N. and Hamzah, M. I. M. (2017). 'Mentoring and coaching practices for beginner teachers-a need for mentor coaching skills training and principal's support', *Creative Education*, 8(1), pp. 156–69.

Whitmore, J. (2009). 'Coaching for performance: GROWing human potential and purpose: The principles and practice of coaching and leadership', in *People skills for professionals*. 4th edn. Boston, MA: Nicholas Brealey.

Chapter 2 The Professional Self and Psychology

James Boyle, Jeremy Monsen and Lisa Marks Woolfson

Akar, H. and Üstüner, M. (2017). 'Mediation role of self-efficacy perceptions in the relationship between emotional intelligence levels and social entrepreneurship traits of pre-service teachers', *Journal of Education and Future*, 12, pp. 95–115.

Alam, A. and Ahmad, M. (2018). 'The role of teachers' emotional intelligence in enhancing student achievement', *Journal of Asia Business Studies*, 12(1), pp. 31–43. doi:10.1108/jabs-08-2015-0134.

Bakhtin, M. M. (1981). *The dialogic imagination: Four essays by M. M. Bakhtin*. Translated by Emerson, C. and Holquist, M. Austin: University of Texas Press.

Bandura, A. (1977). 'Self-efficacy: Toward a unifying theory of behavioral change', *Psychological Review*, 84(2), pp. 191–215.

Bandura, A. (1986). *Social foundations of thought and action: A social cognitive theory*. Englewood Cliffs, NJ: Prentice-Hall.

Barron, I. (2016). 'Flight turbulence: The stormy professional trajectory of trainee early years' teachers in England', *International Journal of Early Years Education*, 24(3), pp. 325–41. doi:10.1080/09669760.2016.1204906.

Bates, B. (2019). *Learning theories simplified … and how to apply them to teaching*. 2nd edn. London: Sage.

Beijaard, D., Meijer, P. C. and Verloop, N. (2004). 'Reconsidering research on teachers' professional identity', *Teaching and Teacher Education*, 20(2), pp. 107–28. doi:10.1016/j.tate.2003.07.001.

Black, K. (2008). 'Teacher? The changing professional identity of teachers and the "Every child matters" agenda', *British Educational Research Association Annual Conference*, Heriot-Watt University, Edinburgh, 3–6 September 2008.

Braun, V. and Clarke, V. (2006). 'Using thematic analysis in psychology', *Qualitative Research in Psychology*, 3(2), pp. 77–101. doi:10.1191/1478088706qp063oa.

Brooke, G. E. (1994). 'My personal journey toward professionalism', *Young Children*, 49(6), pp. 69–71.

Brownell, M. T., Bishop, A. G., Gersten, R., Klingner, J. K., Penfield, R. D., Dimino, J., Haager, D., Menon, S. and Sindelar, P. T. (2009). 'The role of domain expertise in beginning special education teacher quality', *Exceptional Children*, 75(4), pp. 391–411.

Butler, D. L., Lauscher, H. N., Jarvis-Selinger, S. and Beckingham, B. (2004). 'Collaboration and self-regulation in teachers' professional development', *Teaching and Teacher Education*, 20(5), pp. 435–55. doi:10.1016/j.tate.2004.04.003.

Canrinus, E. T., Helms-Lorenz, M., Beijaard, D., Buitink, J. and Hofman, A. (2011). 'Self-efficacy, job satisfaction, motivation and commitment: Exploring the relationships between indicators of teachers' professional identity', *European Journal of Psychology of Education*, 27(1), pp. 115–32. doi:10.1007/s10212-011-0069-2

Canter, L. and Canter, M. (1992). *Assertive discipline*. Los Angeles, CA: Canter and Associates.

Castells, M. (2010). *The power of identity*. 2nd edn. Chichester, West Sussex: Wiley-Blackwell.

Casteneda, J. A. F. (2011). *Teacher identity construction: Exploring the nature of becoming a primary language teacher*. PhD Thesis. Newcastle University. Available at: https://core.ac.uk/download/pdf/40013454.pdf (accessed 23 March 2020).

Castle, P. and Buckler, S. (2018). *Psychology for teachers*. 2nd edn. London: Sage.

Chong, S., Low, E. L. and Goh, K. C. (2011). 'Developing student teachers' professional identities – An exploratory study', *International Education Studies*, 4(1). doi:10.5539/ies.v4n1p30.

Cline, T. (2015a). 'Effective communication in school: Do teachers and students talk the same language?' in Cline, T., Gulliford, A. and Birch, S. (eds.) *Educational psychology: Topics in applied psychology*. 2nd edn. London: Routledge, pp. 134–54.

Cline, T. (2015b). 'School ethos and school identity: When is wearing a uniform a badge of honour?' in Cline, T., Gulliford, A. and Birch, S. (eds.) *Educational psychology: Topics in applied psychology*. 2nd edn. London: Routledge, pp. 306–21.

Cohen, J. A., Heath, M. A., Hudnall, G. and Mannarino, A. P. (2011). 'Supporting children with traumatic grief: What educators need to know', *School Psychology International*, 32(2), pp. 117–31. doi:10.1177/0143034311400827.

Conderman, G. and Johnston-Rodriguez, S. (2009). 'Beginning teachers' views of their collaborative roles', *Preventing School Failure: Alternative Education for Children and Youth*, 53(4), pp. 235–44. doi:10.3200/psfl.53.4.235-244.

Cordingley, P., Crisp, B., Johns, O., Perry, T., Campbell, C., Bell, M. and Bradbury, M. (2019). *Constructing teachers' professional identities: Learning from 7 jurisdictions*. Brussels, Belgium: Education International.

Darby, A. (2008). 'Teachers' emotions in the reconstruction of professional self-understanding', *Teaching and Teacher Education*, 24(5), pp. 1160–72. doi:10.1016/j.tate.2007.02.001.

Day, C., Kington, A., Stobart, G. and Sammons, P. (2006). 'The personal and professional selves of teachers: Stable and unstable identities', *British Educational Research Journal*, 32(4), pp. 601–16. doi:10.1080/01411920600775316.

Department for Education (Northern Ireland). (2018). *Dealing with a critical incident*. Available at: https://www.eani.org.uk/sites/default/files/2018-09/Guide%20to%20Managing%20Critical%20Incidents%20in%20Schools.pdf (accessed 23 March 2020).

Erikson, E. H. (1968). *Identity, youth and crisis*. New York: W. W. Norton.

Espelage, D. L., Hong, J. S., Merrin, G. J., Davis, J. P., Rose, C. A. and Little, T. D. (2018). 'A longitudinal examination of homophobic name-calling in middle school: Bullying, traditional masculinity, and sexual harassment as predictors', *Psychology of Violence*, 8(1), pp. 57–66. doi:10.1037/vio0000083.

Eton Institute. (n.d.). *The 7 roles of a teacher in the 21st century*. Available at: https://etoninstitute.com/blog/the-7-roles-of-a-teacher-in-the-21st-century (accessed 23 March 2020).

Feryok, A. (2009). 'Activity theory, imitation and their role in teacher development', *Language Teaching Research*, 13(3), pp. 279–99.

Friesen, M. D. and Besley, S. C. (2013). 'Teacher identity development in the first year of teacher education: A developmental and social psychological perspective', *Teaching and Teacher Education*, 36, pp. 23–32. doi:10.1016/j.tate.2013.06.005.

Fuchs, L. S., Fuchs, D. and Hamlett, C. L. (1994). 'Strengthening the connection between assessment and instructional planning with expert systems', *Exceptional Children*, 61(2), pp. 138–46.

Fullan, M. and Langworthy, M. (2014). *A rich seam: How new pedagogies find deep learning*. London: Pearson.

Fullan, M., Rincón-Gallardo, S. and Hargreaves, A. (2015). 'Professional capital as accountability', *Educational Policy Analysis Archives*, 23(15), pp. 1–22.

Gerson, M. (2015). *How to use Bloom's Taxonomy in the classroom: The complete guide*. Scotts Valley, CA: CreateSpace Independent Publishing Platform.

Gulliford, A. and Miller, A. (2015). 'Managing classroom behaviour: Perspectives from psychology', in Cline, T., Gulliford, A. and Birch, S. (eds.) *Educational psychology: Topics in applied psychology*. 2nd edn. London: Routledge, pp. 223–57.

Gulliford, A. and Miller, A. (2015a). 'Coping with life by coping with school? School refusal in young children', in Cline, T., Gulliford, A. and Birch, S. (eds.) *Educational psychology: Topics in applied psychology*. 2nd edn. London: Routledge, pp. 283–305.

Guyana Ministry of Education. (n.d.). *Roles of a teacher in the Classroom*. Available at: https://www.education.gov.gy/web/index.php/teachers/tips-for-teaching/item/1603-roles-of-a-teacher-in-the-classroom (accessed 23 March 2020).

Harlow, A. and Cobb, D. (2014). 'Planting the seed of teacher identity: Nurturing early growth through a collaborative learning community', *Australian Journal of Teacher Education*, 39(7). doi:10.14221/ajte.2014v39n7.8.

Harrison, C. and Killion, J. (2013). *Ten roles for teacher leaders*. Available at: https://pdo.ascd.org/LMSCourses/PD13OC010M/media/Leading_Prof_Learning_M2_Reading1.pdf (accessed 23 March 2020).

Hattie, J. (2012). *Visible learning for teachers*. London: Routledge.

Holland, D., Lachicotte, W., Jr., Skinner, D. and Cain, C. (1998). *Identity and agency in cultural worlds*. Cambridge, MA: Harvard University Press.

Holland, J. (2016). *Responding to loss and bereavement in schools*. London: Jessica Kingsley Publishers.

Hong, J. Y. (2010). 'Pre-service and beginning teachers' professional identity and its relation to dropping out of the profession', *Teaching and Teacher Education*, 26(8), pp. 1530–43. doi:10.1016/j.tate.2010.06.003.

Hsieh, B. (2010). *Exploring the complexity of teacher professional identity*. PhD Thesis. University of California, Berkeley. Available at: https://escholarship.org/uc/item/9406p4sb (accessed 23 March 2020).

Hsieh, B. (2015). 'The importance of orientation: Implications of professional identity on classroom practice and for professional learning', *Teachers and Teaching*, 21(2), pp. 178–90. doi:10.1080/13540602.2014.928133.

Ismail, N. A. H. and Tekke, M. (2015). 'Rediscovering Rogers's self theory and personality', *Journal of Educational, Health and Community Psychology*, 4(3), pp. 28–36.

Izadinia, M. (2016). 'Preservice teachers' professional identity development and the role of mentor teachers', *International Journal of Mentoring and Coaching in Education*, 5(2), pp. 127–43. doi:10.1108/ijmce-01-2016-0004.

Jones, W. M. and Dexter, S. (2014). 'How teachers learn: The roles of formal, informal, and independent learning', *Educational Technology Research and Development*, 62(3), pp. 367–84. doi:10.1007/s11423-014-9337-6.

Joyce, B. and Showers, B. (2002). *Student achievement through staff development*. 3rd edn. Alexandria, VA: Association for Supervision and Curriculum Development.

Kanadlı, S. (2017). 'Prospective teachers' professional self-efficacy beliefs in terms of their perceived autonomy support and attitudes towards the teaching profession: A mixed methods study', *Educational Sciences: Theory & Practice*, 17(5), pp. 1847–71. doi:10.12738/estp.2017.5.0597.

Kelchtermans, G. (1993). 'Getting the story, understanding the lives: From career stories to teachers' professional development', *Teaching and Teacher Education*, 9(5–6), pp. 443–56. doi:10.1016/0742-051x(93)90029-g.

Kington, A., Sammons, P., Regan, E., Brown, E., Ko, J. and Buckler, S. (2014). *Effective classroom practice*. Maidenhead: Open University Press.

Klassen, R. M., Tze, V. M. C., Betts, S. M. and Gordon, K. A. (2011). 'Teacher efficacy research 1998–2009: Signs of progress or unfulfilled promise?' *Educational Psychology Review*, 23, pp. 21–43.

Kyriacou, C. (2014). *Effective teaching in schools: Theory and practice*. 4th edn. Oxford: Oxford University Press.

Lambert, N. and Frederickson, N. (2015). 'Inclusion for children with special educational needs: How can psychology help?' in Cline, T., Gulliford, A. and Birch, S. (eds.) *Educational psychology: Topics in applied psychology*. 2nd edn. London: Routledge, pp. 108–33.

Lamote, C. and Engels, N. (2010). 'The development of student teachers' professional identity', *European Journal of Teacher Education*, 33(1), pp. 3–18. doi:10.1080/02619760903457735.

Lauchlan, F. (2003). 'Responding to chronic non-attendance: A review of intervention approaches', *Educational Psychology in Practice*, 19(2), pp. 133–46. doi:10.1080/02667360303236.

Lentillon-Kaestner, V., Guillet-Descas, E., Martinent, G. and Cece, V. (2018). 'Validity and reliability of questionnaire on perceived professional identity among teachers (QIPPE) scores', *Studies in Educational Evaluation*, 59, pp. 235–43. doi:10.1016/j.stueduc.2018.09.003.

Lortie, D. C. (2002). *Schoolteacher: A sociological study*. 2nd edn. Chicago, IL: University of Chicago Press.

Louws, M. L., Meirink, J. A., van Veen, K. and van Driel, J. H. (2017). 'Teachers' self-directed learning and teaching experience: What, how, and why teachers want to learn', *Teaching and Teacher Education*, 66, pp. 171–83. doi:10.1016/j.tate.2017.04.004.

Ma, J. Y. and Singer-Gabella, M. (2011). 'Learning to teach in the figured world of reform mathematics: Negotiating new models of identity', *Journal of Teacher Education*, 62(1), pp. 8–22. doi:10.1177/0022487110378851.

Malderez, A., Hobson, A. J., Tracey, L. and Kerr, K. (2007). 'Becoming a student teacher: Core features of the experience', *European Journal of Teacher Education*, 30(3), pp. 225–48. doi:10.1080/02619760701486068.

McCall, G. J. and Simmons, J. L. (1978). *Identities and interactions*. New York: Free Press.

Mayer, J. D., Salovey, P. and Caruso, D. R. (2004). 'Emotional intelligence: Theory, findings, and implications'. *Psychological Inquiry*, 15(3), pp. 197–215.

Meyer, E. S. (2010). *Gender and sexual diversity in schools: An introduction*. London: Springer.

Mocanu, M., and Sterian, M. (2013). 'Emotional intelligence and teacher's changing role', *Euromentor Journal*, 4(2), pp. 118–27.

Mohr, K. A. J., Juth, S. M., Kohlmeier, T. L. and Schreiber, K. E. (2018). 'The developing bilingual brain: What parents and teachers should know and do', *Early Childhood Education Journal*, 46(1), pp. 11–20. doi:10.1007/s10643-016-0833-7.

Phillippo, K. L. and Stone, S. (2013). 'Teacher role breadth and its relationship to student-reported teacher support', *The High School Journal* (April/May), pp. 358–79.

Reinke, W. M., Stormont, M., Herman, K. C., Puri, R. and Goel, N. (2011). 'Supporting children's mental health in schools: Teacher perceptions of needs, roles, and barriers', *School Psychology Quarterly*, 26(1), pp. 1–13. doi:10.1037/a0022714.

Rogers, B. (2015). *Classroom management behaviour: A practical guide to effective teaching behaviour management and colleague support.* 4th edn. London: Sage.

Rogers, C. R. (1961). *On becoming a person: A therapist's view of psychotherapy.* Boston: Houghton-Mifflin.

Ruohotie-Lyhty, M. and Moate, J. (2016). 'Who and how? Preservice teachers as active agents developing professional identities', *Teaching and Teacher Education*, 55, pp. 318–27. doi:10.1016/j.tate.2016.01.022.

Ryan, R. M, and Deci, E. L. (2000). 'Self-determination theory and the facilitation of intrinsic motivation, social development, and well-being', *American Psychologist*, 55(1), pp. 68–78. doi:10.1037///0003-066X.55.1.68.

Sammons, P., Day, C., Kington, A., Gu, Q., Stobart, G. and Smees, R. (2007). 'Exploring variations in teachers' work, lives and their effects on pupils: Key findings and implications from a longitudinal mixed method study', *British Educational Research Journal*, 33(5), pp. 681–701. doi:10.1080/01411920701582264.

SchoolNet SA. (2000). *Norms and standards for educators.* Available at: http://academic.sun.ac.za/mathed/174/NORMS%20AND%20STANDARDS%20FOR%20EDUCATORS.pdf (accessed 23 March 2020).

Scottish Government. (2019). *Review of personal and social education: Preparing Scotland's children and young people for learning, work and life.* Available at: https://www.gov.scot/publications/review-personal-social-education-preparing-scotlands-children-young-people-learning-work-life/ (accessed 23 March 2020).

Smith, P. K. (2016). 'Bullying: Definition, types, causes, consequences and intervention', *Social and Personality Psychology Compass*, 10(9), pp. 519–32. doi:10.1111/spc3.12266.

Stets, J. E. and Burke, P. J. (2000). 'Identity theory and social identity theory', *School Psychology Quarterly*, 63(3), pp. 224–37.

Steyn, G. M. (2018). 'The impact of school context on the construction of female mathematic teachers' professional identity in a South African primary school', *Pertanika Journal of Social Sciences & Humanities*, 26(1), pp. 519–34.

Stryker, S. and Burke, P. J. (2000). 'The past, present, and future of an identity theory', *Social Psychology Quarterly*, 63(4), pp. 284–97. doi:10.2307/2695840.

Summers, J. J., Davis, H. A. and Woolfolk Hoy, A. (2017). 'The effects of teachers' efficacy beliefs on student perceptions of teacher relationship quality', *Learning and Individual Differences*, 53, pp. 17–25.

Tajfel, H. E. (1978). *Differentiation between social groups: Studies in the social psychology of intergroup relations.* London: Academic Press.

Tajfel, H. E. and Turner, J. C. (2004). 'The social identity theory of intergroup behavior', in Jost, J. T. and Sidanius, J. (eds.) *Key readings in social psychology. Political psychology: Key readings*. London: Psychology Press, pp. 276–93.

TEACH. (n.d.). *What does a teacher do?* Available at: https://teach.com/what/ (accessed 23 March 2020).

Teasley, M. L. (2017). 'Organizational culture and schools: A call for leadership and collaboration', *Children & Schools*, 39(1), pp. 3–6.

Timoštšuk, I. and Ugaste, A. (2010). 'Student teachers' professional identity', *Teaching and Teacher Education*, 26(8), pp. 1563–70. doi:10.1016/j.tate.2010.06.008.

Ttofi, M. M. and Farrington, D. P. (2010). 'Effectiveness of school-based programs to reduce bullying: A systematic and meta-analytic review', *Journal of Experimental Criminology*, 7(1), pp. 27–56. doi:10.1007/s11292-010-9109-1.

Urrieta, L. (2007). 'Figured worlds and education: An introduction to the special issue', *The Urban Review*, 39(2), pp. 107–16. doi:10.1007/s11256-007-0051-0.

Varghese, M. M. and Snyder, R. (2018). 'Critically examining the agency and professional identity development of novice dual language teachers through figured worlds', *International Multilingual Research Journal*, 12(3), pp. 145–59. doi:10.1080/19313152.2018.1474060.

Vygotsky, L. S. (1978). *Mind in society: The development of higher psychological processes*. Cole, M., John-Steine, V., Scribner, S. and Souberman, E. (eds.). Translated by Luria, A. R., Lopez-Morillas, C. M. and Wertsch, J. V. Cambridge, MA: Harvard University Press.

Woolfolk Hoy, A. (2000). *Changes in teacher efficacy during the early years of teaching*. Paper presented at the Annual Meeting of the American Educational Research Association, New Orleans, Session 43:22, 28 April.

Zee, M. and Koomen, H. M. Y. (2016). 'Teacher self-efficacy and its effects on classroom processes, student academic adjustment, and teacher well-being', *Review of Educational Research*, 86, pp. 981–1015.

Chapter 3 Health and Well-Being in Psychology

Lisa Marks Woolfson and Stuart Woodcock

Bandura, A. (1977). 'Self-efficacy: Toward a unifying theory of behavioral change', *Psychological Review*, 84(2), pp. 191–215.

Bandura, A. (1997). *Self-efficacy: The exercise of control*. New York: Macmillan.

Beauchamp, C. and Thomas, L. (2009). 'Understanding teacher identity: An overview of issues in the literature and implications for teacher education', *Cambridge Journal of Education*, 39(2), pp. 175–89.

Beijaard, D., Meijer, P. C. and Verloop, N. (2004). 'Reconsidering research on teachers' professional identity', *Teaching and Teacher Education*, 20(2), pp. 107–28.

Bergami, M. and Bagozzi, R. P. (2000). 'Self categorization, affective commitment and group self esteem as distinct aspects of social identity in the organization', *British Journal of Social Psychology*, 39(4), pp. 555–77.

Brady, K. and Woolfson, L. (2008). 'What teacher factors influence their attributions for children's difficulties in learning?' *British Journal of Educational Psychology*, 78, pp. 527–44.

Danna, K. and Griffin, R. W. (1999). 'Health and well-being in the workplace: A review and synthesis of the literature', *Journal of Management*, 25(3), pp. 357–84.

Dicke, T. et al. (2015). 'Reducing reality shock: The effects of classroom management skills training on beginning teachers', *Teaching and Teacher Education*, 48, pp. 1–12.

Gu, Q. and Day, C. (2007). 'Teachers resilience: A necessary condition for effectiveness', *Teaching and Teacher Education*, 23(8), pp. 1302–16.

Hong, J. Y. (2012). 'Why do some beginning teachers leave the school, and others stay? Understanding teacher resilience through psychological lenses', *Teachers and Teaching*, 18(4), pp. 417–40.

Izadinia, M. (2015). 'A closer look at the role of mentor teachers in shaping preservice teachers' professional identity', *Teaching and Teacher Education*, 52, pp. 1–10.

Jennings, P. and DeMauro, A. (2017). 'Individual-level interventions: Mindfulness-based approaches to reducing stress and improving performance among teachers', in McIntyre, T., McIntyre, S. and Francis, D. (eds.) *Educator stress: An occupational health perspective*. New York: Springer International Publishing, pp. 319–46.

Kyriacou, C. (2001). 'Teacher stress: Directions for future research', *Educational Review*, 53(1), pp. 27–35.

Le Cornu, R. (2009). 'Building resilience in pre-service teachers', *Teaching and Teacher Education*, 25(5), pp. 717–23.

Lunenburg, F. C. (2011). 'Self-efficacy in the workplace: Implications for motivation and performance', *International Journal of Management, Business, and Administration*, 14(1), pp. 1–6.

Marek, T., Schaufeli, W. B. and Maslach, C. (2017). *Professional burnout: Recent developments in theory and research*. Abingdon, Oxford: Routledge.

Naghieh, A. et al. (2015). 'Organisational interventions for improving wellbeing and reducing work-related stress in teachers', *Cochrane Database of Systematic Reviews*, 4(4).

O'Connor, K. E. (2008). '"You choose to care": Teachers, emotions and professional identity', *Teaching and Teacher Education*, 24(1), pp. 117–26.

Papastylianou, A., Kaila, M. and Polychronopoulos, M. (2009). 'Teachers' burnout, depression, role ambiguity and conflict', *Social Psychology of Education*, 12(3), pp. 295–314.

Pearson, L. C. and Moomaw, W. (2006). 'Continuing validation of the teaching autonomy scale', *The Journal of Educational Research*, 100(1), pp. 44–51.

Pitt, A. and Phelan, A. (2008). 'Paradoxes of autonomy in professional life: A research problem', *Changing English*, 15(2), pp. 189–97.

Rogers, C. (2002). 'The interpersonal relationship in the facilitation of learning', in Harrison, R. et al. (eds.) *Supporting lifelong learning: Perspectives on learning* (Vol. 1). London: Routledge, pp. 25–39.

Royer, N. and Moreau, C. (2016). 'A survey of Canadian early childhood educators' psychological wellbeing at work', *Early Childhood Education Journal*, 44(2), pp. 135–46.

Schwab, R. L. and Iwanicki, E. F. (1982). 'Perceived role conflict, role ambiguity, and teacher burnout', *Educational Administration Quarterly*, 18(1), pp. 60–74.

Spector, P. E. (1986). 'Perceived control by employees: A meta-analysis of studies concerning autonomy and participation at work', *Human Relations*, 39(11), pp. 1005–16.

Tajfel, H. et al. (1971). 'Social categorization and intergroup behaviour', *European Journal of Social Psychology*, 1(2), pp. 149–78.

Weiner, B. (1985). 'An attributional theory of achievement motivation and emotion', *Psychological Review*, 92(4), pp. 548–73.

Wheatley, D. (2017). 'Autonomy in paid work and employee subjective well-being', *Work and Occupations*, 44(3), pp. 296–328.

Wilson, C., Woolfson, L. M. and Durkin, K. (2020). 'School environment and mastery experience as predictors of teachers' self-efficacy beliefs towards inclusive teaching', *International Journal of Inclusive Education*, 24(2), pp. 218–234.

Chapter 4 The Social World of the Classroom

Matthew P. Somerville and Ed Baines

Adey, P. (2012). 'From fixed IQ to multiple intelligences', in Adey, P. and Dillon, J. (eds.) *Bad Education: Debunking Myths in Education*. Maidenhead, UK: Open University Press, pp. 199–214.

Ainsworth, M. D. S. and Bowlby, J. (1991). 'An ethological approach to personality development', *American Psychologist*, 46, pp. 331–41.

Alexander, R. (2004). *Towards dialogic teaching: Rethinking classroom talk*. 2nd edn. London, UK: Dialogis.

Archer, L., Francis, B., Miller, S., Taylor, B., Tereshchenko, A., Mazenod, A. and Travers, M-C. (2018). 'The symbolic violence of setting: A Bourdieusian analysis of mixed methods data on secondary students' views about setting', *British Educational Research Journal*, 44, pp. 119–40.

Babad, E. (2009). *The social psychology of the classroom*. Abingdon, UK: Routledge.

Baines, E. (2020). 'Ability grouping', in Hattie, J. and Anderman, E. M. (eds.) *Visible learning guide to student achievement: Schools edition*. Abingdon, OX: Routledge, pp. 79–85.

Baines, E. and Howe, C. (2010). 'Discourse topic management skills in 4-, 6- and 9-year-old peer interactions: Developments with age and the effects of task context', *First Language*, 30, pp. 508–35.

Baines, E., Blatchford, P. and Kutnick, P. (2003). 'Grouping practices in classrooms: Changing patterns over primary and secondary schooling', *International Journal of Educational Research*, 39, pp. 9–34.

Baines, E., Rubie-Davies, C. and Blatchford, P. (2009). 'Improving pupil group work interaction and dialogue in primary classrooms: Results from a year-long intervention study', *Cambridge Journal of Education*, 39, pp. 95–117.

Baines, E., Blatchford, P. and Kutnick, P. (2016). *Promoting effective group work in the primary classroom: A handbook for teachers and practitioners*. 2nd edn. London: Routledge.

Blatchford, P. and Russell, A. (2020). *Rethinking Class size: The complex story of impact and what it means for teaching*. London: UCL Press.

Blatchford, P., Kutnick, P., Baines, E. and Galton, M. (2003). 'Toward a social pedagogy of classroom group work', *International Journal of Educational Research*, 39, pp. 153–72.

Blatchford, P., Galton, M., Kutnick, P., Baines, E. and Pell, A. (2005). *Improving pupil group work in classrooms: A new approach to increasing engagement and learning in everyday classroom settings at Key Stages 1, 2 and 3*. Final Report to ESRC.

Blatchford, P., Bassett, P., Brown, P. and Webster, R. (2009). 'The effect of support staff on pupil engagement and individual attention', *British Educational Research Journal*, 35, pp. 661–86.

Blatchford, P., Pellegrini, A., and Baines, E. (2016). *The child at school: Interactions with peers and teachers. (2nd edition)*. London, UK: Routledge.

Brophy, J. and Good, T. (1986). 'Naturalistic studies of teacher expectation effects', in Hammersley, M. (ed.) *Case studies in classroom research*. Milton Keynes: Open University, pp. 210–30.

Cazden, C. B. (2001). *Classroom discourse: The language of teaching and learning*. 2nd edn. Portsmouth, NH: Heinemann.

Cooper, H. M. (1985). 'Models of teacher expectation communication', in Dusek, J. B. (ed.) *Teacher expectancies*. London: Erlbaum, pp. 135–58.

Doise, W. and Mugny, G. (1984). 'The social development of the intellect', *International Series in Experimental Social Psychology*, 10. Pergamon Press.

Dunne, M., Humphreys, S., Dyson, A., Sebba, J., Gallannaugh, F. and Muijs, D. (2011). 'The teaching and learning of pupils in low-attainment sets', *Curriculum Journal*, 22, pp. 485–513.

Epstein, J. L. (1983). 'The influence of friends on achievement and affective outcomes', in Epstein, J. L. and Karweit, N. (eds.) *Friends in school: Patterns of selection and influence in secondary schools*. New York: Academic Press, pp. 177–200.

Flanders, N. A. and Havumaki, S. (1960). 'The effect of teacher-pupil contacts involving praise on the sociometric choices of students', *Journal of Educational Psychology*, 57, pp. 65–8.

Galton, M. and Williamson, J. (1992). *Group work in the primary classroom*. London: Routledge.

Galton, M., Hargreaves, L., Comber, C., Wall, D. and Pell, T. (1999). 'Changes in patterns of teacher interaction in primary classrooms: 1976–96', *British Educational Research Journal*, 25, pp. 23–37.

Gillies, R. M. and Boyle, M. (2010). 'Teachers' reflections on cooperative learning: Issues of implementation', *Teaching and Teacher Education*, 26, pp. 933–40.

Hallinan, M. T. and Kubitschek, W. N. (1999). 'Curriculum differentiation and high school achievement', *Social Psychology of Education*, 2, pp. 1–22.

Hattie, J. (2016). 'The right question in the debates about class size', in Blatchford, P., Chan, K. W., Galton, M., Lai, K. C. and Lee, J. C. K. (eds.) *Class size: Eastern and Western perspectives*. Abingdon, UK: Routledge, pp. 105–18.

Howe, C. (2010). *Peer Groups and Children's Development*. Oxford, UK: Wiley Blackwell.

Howe, C. and Tolmie, A. (2003). 'Group work in primary school science: Discussion, consensus and guidance from experts', *International Journal of Educational Research*, 39, pp. 51–72.

Johnson, D. W. and Johnson, F. (2013). *Joining together: Group theory and research*. Boston, MA: Allyn and Bacon.

Kutnick, P. and Kington, A. (2005). 'Children's friendship and learning in school, cognitive engagement through social interaction', *British Journal of Educational Psychology*, 75, pp. 521–38.

Kutnick, P. and Blatchford, P. with Baines, E. and Tolmie, A. (2014). *Effective group work in primary school classrooms: The SPRinG approach*. London: Springer.

Luckin, R., Baines, E., Cukurova, M., Holmes, W. and Mann, M. (2017). *Solved! Making the case for collaborative problem-solving*. Available at: https://www.nesta.org.uk/report/solved-making-the-case-for-collaborative-problem-solving/

Luthar, S. S., Cicchetti, D. and Becker, B. (2000). 'The construct of resilience: A critical evaluation and guidelines for future work', *Child Development*, 71, pp. 543–62.

Mercer, N., Hennessy, S. and Warwick, P. (2017). 'Dialogue, thinking together and digital technology in the classroom: Some educational implications of a continuing line of inquiry', *International Journal of Educational Research*, 97, pp. 187–99.

Monsen, J. J. and Frederickson, N. (2004). 'Teachers' attitudes towards mainstreaming and their pupils' perceptions of their classroom learning environment', *Learning Environments Research*, 7, pp. 129–42.

Nuthall, G. (2007). *The hidden lives of learners*. Wellington, New Zealand: NZCER Press.

Oakes, J. (2005). *Keeping track: How schools structure inequality*. New Haven, CT: Yale University Press.

Obiakor, F. E. (1999). 'Teacher expectations of minority exceptional learners: Impact on accuracy of self-concepts', *Exceptional Children*, 66, pp. 39–53.

OECD. (2012). *Equity and quality in education: Supporting disadvantaged students and schools*. OECD Publishing. Available at: http://dx.doi.org/10.1787/9789264130852-en.

Pianta, R. C. (2001). *Student teacher relationship scale: Professional manual*. Lutz, FL: Psychological Assessment Resources.

Pianta, R. C. and Nimetz, S. L. (1991). 'Relationships between children and teachers: Associations with classroom and home behavior', *Journal of Applied Developmental Psychology*, 12, pp. 379–93.

Pianta, R. C., Hamre, B. and Stuhlman, M. (2003). 'Relationships between teachers and children', in Reynolds, W. M. and Miller, G. E. (eds.) *Handbook of psychology: Educational psychology* (Vol. 7). Hoboken, NJ: Wiley, pp. 199–234.

Radford, J., Blatchford, P. and Webster, R. (2011). 'Opening up and closing down: How teachers and TAs manage turn-taking, topic and repair in mathematics lessons', *Learning and Instruction*, 21, pp. 625–35.

Reeve, J. (2002). 'Self-determination theory applied to educational settings', in Deci, E. L. and Ryan, R. M. (eds.) *Handbook of self-determination research*. Rochester, NY: University of Rochester Press, pp. 183–203.

Riegle-Crumb, C., and Humphries, M. (2012). 'Exploring bias in math teachers' perceptions of students' ability by gender and race/ethnicity', *Gender and Society*, 26, pp. 290–322.

Riley, K. A. (2004). 'Schooling the citizens of tomorrow: The challenges for teaching and learning across the global north/south divide'. *Journal of Educational Change*, 5, pp. 389–415.

Rosenthal, R. and Jacobson, L. (1968). *Pygmalion in the classroom: Teacher expectation and pupils' intellectual development*. New York: Holt, Rinehart and Winston.

Rubie-Davies, C., Hattie, J. and Hamilton, R. (2010). 'Expecting the best for students: Teacher expectations and academic outcomes', *British Journal of Educational Psychology*, 76, pp. 429–44.

Sabol, T. J. and Pianta, R. C. (2012). 'Recent trends in research on teacher–child relationships', *Attachment and Human Development*, 14, pp. 213–31.

Schofield, J. W. (2010). 'International evidence on ability grouping with curriculum differentiation and the achievement gap in secondary schools', *Teachers College Record*, 112, pp. 1492–528.

Slavin, R. E., Lake, C., Hanley, P. and Thurston, A. (2014). 'Experimental evaluations of elementary science programs: A best-evidence synthesis', *Journal of Research in Science Teaching*. 51, pp. 870–901.

Warrington, P. (2017). *Teaching and learning practices and reported experiences of teachers and students in high, middle and low ability maths classes*. Doctoral dissertation. University College London, Institute of Education. Available at: https://discovery.ucl.ac.uk/id/eprint/1575475/1/PW%20Thesis%20.pdf

Webb, N. M., Franke, M. L., Ing, M., Turrou, A. C., Johnson, N. C. and Zimmerman, J. (2017). 'Teacher practices that promote productive dialogue and learning in mathematics classrooms', *International Journal of Educational Research*, 97, pp. 176–86.

Weinstein, R. S. (2009). *Reaching higher: The power of expectations in schooling*. Cambridge, MA: Harvard University Press.

Wentzel, K. (2009). 'Peers and academic functioning at school', in Rubin, K. H., Bukowski, W. M. and Laursen, B. (eds.) *Handbook of peer interactions, relationships and groups*. New York: Guilford Press, pp. 531–47.

Wiliam, D. and Bartholomew, H. (2004). 'It's not which school but which set you're in that matters: The influence of ability grouping practices on student progress in mathematics', *British Educational Research Journal*, 30, pp. 279–95.

Zajac, R. J. and Hartup, W. W. (1997). Friends as coworkers: Research review and classroom implications', *The Elementary School Journal*, 98, pp. 3–13.

Chapter 5 Effective Interpersonal Communication

Jeremy Monsen, Linda Crichton and Julie Shaw

Arygris, C. and Schön, D. A. (1974). *Theory into practice*. San Francisco, CA: Jossey-Bass.

Arygris, C. and Schön, D. A. (1996). *Organisational learning II: Theory, method and practice*. Reading, MA: Addison Wesley.

Blatchford, P., Pellergrini, A. D. and Baines, E. (2016). *The child at school: Interactions with peers and teachers*. 2nd edn. London: Routledge Taylor and Francis Group.

Cameron, R. J. and Monsen, J. J. (1998). 'Coaching and critical dialogue in educational psychology practice', *Educational and Child Psychology*, 15(4), pp. 112–26.

Croll, P. and Moses, D. (1985). *One in five. The assessment and incidence of special educational needs*. London: Routledge and Kagan Paul.

Lichtenberg, J. W. (1997). 'Expertise in counselling psychology: A concept in search of support', *Educational Psychology Review*, 9(3), pp. 221–38.

Robinson, V. (1998a). *Enhancing practice based learning through critical dialogue*. Workshop for the University of Technology, Sydney, 12 March.

Robinson, V. (1998b). 'Methodology and the research-practice gap', *Educational Researcher*, 27(1), pp. 17–26.

Robinson, V. (1993). *Problem based methodology: Research for the improvement of practice*. Oxford: Pergamon.

Robinson, V. (2014). 'Single and double loop learning', in Phillips, D. (ed.) *Encyclopedia of educational theory and philosophy*. Thousand Oaks, CA: Sage, pp. 754–56.

Robinson, V. (2018). *Reduce change to increase improvement*. Corwin, CA: Sage.

Schein, E. H. (1972). *Professional education: Some new directions*. New York: McGraw-Hill.

Slotte, S. and Hämäläinen, R. P. (2015). 'Decision structuring dialogue', *EURO Journal on Decision Processes*, 3(1–2), pp. 141–59.

Chapter 6 Resilience, Reflection and Reflexivity

James Boyle and Elizabeth King

Ainsworth, M. D. S., Blehar, M. C., Walters, E. and Wall, S. (1978). *Patterns of attachment: A psychological study of the strange situation*. Hillsdale, NJ: Lawrence Erlbaum Associates.

Ainsworth, S. and Oldfield, J. (2019). 'Quantifying teacher resilience: Context matters', *Teaching and Teacher Education*, 82, pp. 117–28.

Akbari, R., Kiany, G. R., Naeeni, M. I. and Allvar, N. K. (2008). 'Teachers' teaching styles, sense of efficacy and reflectivity as correlates of students' achievement outcomes', *Iranian Journal of Applied Linguistics*, 11, pp. 1–28.

Ananiadou, K. and Claro, M. (2009). *21st century skills and competences for new millennium learners in OECD countries*. OECD Education Working Papers, No. 41 Paris: OECD Publishing.

Archer, M. (2012). *The reflexive imperative in late modernity*. Cambridge: Cambridge University Press.

Arnau-Soler, A., Adams, M. J., Clarke, T. K., Macintyre, D. J., Milburn, K., Navrady, L., Hayward, C., Mcintosh, A. and Thomson, P. A. (2019). 'A validation of the diathesis-stress model for depression in Generation Scotland', *Translational Psychiatry*, 9, p. 25. doi:10.1038/s41398-018-0356-7.

Arslan, G. (2019). 'Exploring the effects of positive psychological strengths on psychological adjustment in adolescents', *Child Indicators Research*, 12, pp. 1449–64.

Bakermans-Kranenburg, M. J. and Van Ijzendoorn, M. H. (2009). 'The first 10,000 adult attachment interviews: Distributions of adult attachment representations in clinical and non-clinical groups', *Attachment and Human Development*, 11, pp. 223–63. doi: 10.1080/14616730902814762.

Baron, R. M. and Kenny, D. A. (1986). 'The moderator-mediator variable distinction in social psychological research: Conceptual, strategic, and statistical considerations', *Journal of Personality and Social Psychology*, 51, pp. 1173–82.

Beltman, S., Mansfield, C. and Price, A. (2011). 'Thriving not just surviving: A review of research on teacher resilience', *Educational Research Review*, 6, pp. 185–207.

Berger, K. S. (2015). *The developing person through the life span*. 10th edn. New York: Worth Publishers.

Blair, B. L., Perry, N. B., O'Brien, M., Calkins, S. D., Keane, S. P. and Shanahan, L. (2015). 'Identifying developmental cascades among differentiated dimensions of social competence and emotion regulation', *Developmental Psychology*, 51, pp. 1062–73.

Bolton, G. (2010). *Reflective practice: Writing and professional development*. London: Sage.

Booth, A., Carver, K. and Granger, D. A. (2000). 'Biosocial perspectives on the family', *Journal of Marriage and the Family*, 62, pp. 1018–34.

Bourdieu, P. (2004). *Science of science and reflexivity*. Cambridge: Polity Press.

Bowlby, J. (1969). *Attachment and loss. Volume one: Attachment*. New York: Basic Books.

Bowlby, J. (1982). 'Attachment and loss: Retrospect and prospect', *American Journal of Orthopsychiatry*, 52, pp. 664–78.

Brody, S. (1981). 'The concepts of attachment and bonding', *Journal of the American Psychoanalytic Association*, 29, pp. 815–29.

Brookfield, S. (1998). 'Critically reflective practice', *The Journal of Continuing Education in the Health Professions*, 18, pp. 197–205.

Brunetti, G. J. (2006). 'Resilience under fire: Perspectives on the work of experienced, inner city high school teachers in the United States', *Teaching and Teacher Education*, 22, pp. 812–25.

Bunce, M. and Rickards, A. (2004). *Working with bereaved children: A guide*. Colchester, Essex: Children's Legal Centre.

Burns, J., Jr. (2008). *The new 3rs in education: Respect, responsibility & relationships*. Charleston, SC: Booksurge Publishing.

Burr, V. (2003). *Social constructionism*. London: Routledge.

Castle, P. and Buckler, S. (2018). *Psychology for teachers*. London: Sage.

Coan, J. A. (2008). 'Towards a neuroscience of attachment', in Cassidy, J. and Shaver, P. R. (eds.) *The handbook of attachment: Theory, research, and clinical implications*. 2nd edn. New York: The Guildford Press, pp. 241–65.

Cozolino, L. (2013). *The social neuroscience of education: Optimizing attachment and learning in the classroom*. New York: W. W. Norton.

Dewey, J. (1933). *How we think*. Buffalo, NY: Prometheus Books.

Duarte, F. and Fitzgerald, A. (2006). 'Guiding principles for a reflexive approach to teaching organisation studies', *Journal of University Teaching & Learning Practice*, 3. Available at: http://ro.uow.edu.au/jutlp/vol3/iss1/3 (accessed 23 March 2020).

Education Support Partnership. (2018). *Teacher Wellbeing Index 2018*. Available at: https://www.educationsupport.org.uk/resources/research-reports/teacher-wellbeing-index-2018 (accessed 23 March 2020).

Eraut, M. (1995). 'Schön shock: A case for reframing reflection in action', *Teachers and teaching*, 1, pp. 9–22.

Feucht, F. C., Lunn Brownlee, J. and Schraw, G. (2017). 'Moving beyond reflection: Reflexivity and epistemic cognition in teaching and teacher education', *Educational Psychologist*, 52, pp. 234–41.

Fonagy, P. and Target, M. (2002). 'Early intervention and the development of self-regulation', *Psychoanalytic Inquiry*, 22, pp. 307–35.

Fong, M. C., Measelle, J., Conradt, E. and Ablow, J. C. (2017). 'Links between early baseline cortisol, attachment classification, and problem behaviors: A test of differential susceptibility versus diathesis-stress', *Infant Behavior and Development*, 46, pp. 158–68.

Fook, J. (2007). 'Reflective practice and critical reflection', in Lishman, J. (ed.) *Handbook for practice learning in social work and social care: Second edition: Knowledge and theory*. London: Jessica Kingsley, pp. 363–75.

Garza, R. and Smith, S. F. (2015). 'Pre-service teachers' blog reflections: Illuminating their growth and development', *Cogent Education*, 2, pp. 1–15.

Gazelle, H. and Ladd, G. W. (2003). 'Anxious solitude and peer exclusion: A diathesis-stress model of internalizing trajectories in childhood', *Child Development*, 74, pp. 257–78.

Giddens, A. (1991). *Modernity and self-identity: Self and society in the late modern age*. Stanford, CA: Stanford University Press.

Harlow, E. (2019). 'Attachment theory: developments, debates and recent applications in social work, social care and education'. *Journal of Social Work Practice*, pp. 1–13. doi:10.1080/02650533.2019.1700493

Hibbert, P., Coupland, C. and Macintosh, R. (2010). 'Reflexivity: Recursion and relationality in organizational research processes', *Qualitative Research in Organizations and Management: An International Journal*, 5, pp. 47–62.

Howe, D. (1995). 'Adoption and attachment', *Adoption & Fostering*, 19, pp. 7–15.

Hunter, S. and Boyle, J. (2004). 'Appraisal and coping strategy use in victims of bullying', *British Journal of Educational Psychology*, 74, pp. 83–107.

Kirschman, K. J. B., Johnson, R. J., Bender, J. A. and Roberts, M. C. (2009). 'Positive psychology for children and adolescents: Development, prevention, and promotion', in Lopez, S. J. and Snyder, C. R. (eds.) *The Oxford handbook of positive psychology*. 2nd edn. Oxford: Oxford University Press, pp. 132–48.

Kolb, D.A. (1984). *Experiential learning: Experience as the source of learning and development*. Englewood Cliffs, NJ: Prentice Hall.

Kraemer, S. (1999). 'Promoting resilience: Changing concepts of parenting and child care', *International Journal of Child and Family Welfare*, 3, pp. 273–87.

Larrivee, B. (2008). 'Development of a tool to assess teachers' levels of reflective practice', *Reflective Practice*, 9, pp. 341–60.

Lazarus, R. S. and Folkman, S. (1984). *Stress, appraisal, and coping*. New York: Springer.

Luthar, S. S., Lyman, E. L. and Crossman, E. J. (2014). 'Resilience and positive psychology', in Lewis, M. and Rudolph, K. D. (eds.) *Handbook of developmental psychopathology*. New York: Springer, pp. 125–40. doi:10.1007/978-1-4614-9608-3_7.

Main, M. and Solomon, J. (1990). 'Procedures for identifying disorganized/disoriented infants during the Ainsworth Strange Situation', in Greenberg, M., Cicchetti, D. and Cummings, M. (eds.) *Attachment in the preschool years*. Chicago, IL: University of Chicago Press, pp. 121–60.

Masten, A. S. (2011). 'Resilience in children threatened by extreme adversity: Frameworks for research, practice, and translational synergy', *Developmental Psychopathology*, 23, pp. 493–506.

Masten, A. S. and Cicchetti, D. (2010). 'Developmental cascades', *Developmental Psychopathology*, 22, pp. 491–5.

Masten, A. S. and Obradovic, J. (2006). 'Competence and resilience in development', *Annals of the New York Academy of Science*, 1094, pp. 13–27.

Masten, A. S., Roisman, G. I., Long, J. D., Burt, K. B., Obradovic, J., Riley, J. R., Boelcke-Stennes, K. and Tellegen, A. (2005). 'Developmental cascades: Linking academic achievement and externalizing and internalizing symptoms over 20 years', *Developmental Psychology*, 41, pp. 733–46.

Mesmer, J., Van Ijzendoorn, M. H. and Sagi-Schwartz, A. (2016). 'Cross-cultural patterns of attachment: Universal and contextual dimensions', in Cassidy, J. and Shaver, P. R. (eds.) *Handbook of attachment. Theory, research, and clinical applications*. 3rd edn. New York: The Guilford Press, pp. 852–77.

McCarthy, C. J. (2019). 'Teacher stress: Balancing demands and resources', *Phi Delta Kappan*, 101, pp. 8–14.

OFSTED. (2019). *Teacher well-being at work in schools and further education providers*. Available at: https://www.gov.uk/government/publications/teacher-well-being-at-work-in-schools-and-further-education-providers (accessed 23 March 2020).

Pajares, F. and Urdan, T. (eds.) (2008). *The ones we remember: Scholars reflect on teachers who made a difference*. Charlotte, NC: Information Age Publishing Inc.

Partnership for 21st Century Learning. (2007). *Framework for 21st century learning*. Available at: http://www.p21.org/storage/documents/docs/P21_framework_0116.pdf (accessed 23 March 2020).

Reicher, H. (2010). 'Building inclusive education on social and emotional learning: Challenges and perspectives – A review', *International Journal of Inclusive Education*, 14, pp. 213–46.

Riley, P. J. (2011). *Attachment theory and the teacher-student relationship: A practical guide for teachers, teacher educators and school leaders*. Abingdon, UK: Routledge.

Rogers, C. (2002). 'Defining reflection: Another look at John Dewey and reflective thinking', *Teachers College Record*, 104, pp. 842–66.

Rolfe, G., Freshwater, D. and Japer, M. (2001). *Critical reflection in nursing and the helping professions: A user's guide*. Basingstoke, Hampshire: Palgrave Macmillan.

Rucker, D. D., Preacher, K. J., Tormala, Z. L. and Petty, R. E. (2011). 'Mediation analysis in social psychology: Current practices and new recommendations', *Social and Personality Psychology Compass*, 5, pp. 359–71.

Rutter, M. (2000). 'Resilience reconsidered: Conceptual considerations, empirical findings, and policy implications', in Shonkoff, J. P. and Meisels, S. J. (eds.) *Handbook of early childhood intervention*. 2nd edn. Cambridge: Cambridge University Press, pp. 651–82.

Rutter, M. (2006). 'Implications of resilience concepts for scientific understanding', *Annals of the New York Academy of Science*, 1094, pp. 1–12.

Rutter, M. (2012). 'Resilience as a dynamic concept', *Developmental Psychopathology*, 24, pp. 335–44.

Ryan, M. and Bourke, T. (2013). 'The teacher as reflexive professional: Making visible the excluded discourse in teacher standards', *Discourse: Studies in the Cultural Politics of Education*, 34, pp. 411–23.

Sammons, P., Day, C., Kington, A., Gu, Q., Stobart, G. and Smees, R. (2007). 'Exploring variations in teachers' work, lives and their effects on pupils: Key findings and implications from a longitudinal mixed method study', *British Educational Research Journal*, 33(5), pp. 681–701. doi:10.1080/01411920701582264.

Schaffer, H. R. (2006). *Key concepts in developmental psychology*. London: Sage.

Schön, D. (1983). *The reflective practitioner: How professionals think in action*. London: Temple Smith.

Schön, D. (1987). *Educating the reflective practitioner: Toward a new design for teaching and learning in the professions*. San Francisco, CA: Jossey-Bass Publishers.

Schore, A. N. (2001). 'Effects of a secure attachment relationship on right brain development, affect regulation, and infant mental health', *Infant Mental Health Journal*, 22, pp. 7–66.

Seligman, M. E. P. (2019). 'Positive psychology: A personal history', *Annual Review of Clinical Psychology*, 15, pp. 1–23.

Seligman, M. E. P. and Csikszentmihalyi, M. (2000). 'Positive psychology: An introduction', *American Psychology*, 55, pp. 5–14.

Sigelman, C. K. and Rider, E. A. (2012). *Human development across the life span*. Andover, Hampshire: Wadsworth Cengage Learning.

Simpson, J. A. and Rholes, W. S. (eds.) (2015). *Attachment theory and research: New directions and emerging themes.* New York: The Guilford Press.

Skinner, E. A. and Saxton, E. A. (2019). 'The development of academic coping in children and youth: A comprehensive review and critique', *Developmental Review*, 53. doi:10.1016/j.dr.2019.100870.

Sroufe, L. A., Egeland, B., Carlson, E. A. and Collins, W. A. (2005). *The development of the person: The Minnesota study of risk and adaptation from birth to adulthood.* New York: The Guilford Press.

Steele, H. and Steele, M. (2008). 'Ten clinical uses of the adult attachment interview', in Steele, H. and Steele, M. (eds.) *Clinical applications of the adult attachment interview.* New York: The Guilford Press, pp. 3–30.

Stern, J. A., Fraley, R. C., Jones, J. D., Gross, J. T., Shaver, P. R. and Cassidy, J. (2018). 'Developmental processes across the first two years of parenthood: Stability and change in adult attachment style'. *Dev Psychol*, 54, pp. 975–88.

Sternberg, R. J. (2008). 'Excellence for all', *Educational Leadership*, 66, pp. 14–19.

Stingu, M. M. (2012). 'Reflexive practice in teacher education: Facts and trends', *Procedia – Social and Behavioral Sciences*, 33, pp. 617–21.

Summers, J. J., Davis, H. A. and Woolfolk Hoy, A. (2017). 'The effects of teachers' efficacy beliefs on student perceptions of teacher relationship quality', *Learning and Individual Differences*, 53, pp. 17–25.

Sutton, T. E. (2019). 'Review of attachment theory: Familial predictors, continuity and change, and intrapersonal and relational outcomes', *Marriage & Family Review*, 55, pp. 1–22.

Timbs, J. (ed.) (1825). *The mirror of literature, amusement and instruction.* London: J. Limbird.

Vicedo, M. (2017). 'Putting attachment in its place: Disciplinary and cultural contexts'. *European Journal of Developmental Psychology*, 14, 684–99.

Wagner, T., Kegan, R., Lahey, L., Lemons, R. W., Gawrnier, J., Helsing, D., Howell, A. and Rasmussen, H. T. (2006). *Change leadership: A practical guide to transforming our schools.* San Francisco, CA: Jossey-Bass.

Winkler, A. (2014). 'Resilience as reflexivity: A new understanding for work with looked-after children', *Journal of Social Work Practice*, 28, pp. 461–78.

Yates, T. M., Tyrell, F. and Masten, A. S. (2015). 'Resilience theory and the practice of positive psychology from individuals to societies', in Joseph, S. (ed.) *Positive psychology in practice: Promoting human flourishing in work, health, education, and everyday life.* 2nd edn. Hobokien, NJ: Wiley, pp. 773–88.

Zee, M. and Koomen, H. M. Y. (2016). 'Teacher self-efficacy and its effects on classroom processes, student academic adjustment, and teacher well-being', *Review of Educational Research*, 86, pp. 981–1015.

INDEX

ability grouping of pupils 63, 68
   between classes 64
   within classes 64–5
   forms of 64 (*see also specific forms*)
Accessible Dialogue framework 88–9, 92–3, 98–102, 106, 136
   advocacy 100
   behavioural communication strategies 100–1
   consequences for learning 101–2
   guidelines for learning conversation 102
   Guiding Principles 99
   inferences 100
   interpersonal environment 99–100
   professional development in 103–5
activity theory 29
Adult Attachment Interview (AAI) 110
agency 32, 40, 45, 133
Ahmad, M. 37
Ainsworth, M. D. S. 66
Ainsworth, S. 116
Akbari, R. 123
Alam, A. 37
Alexander, R. 72
appraisal process 112. *See also specific processes*
apprenticeship 20–1
Archer, M. 122
Argyris, C. 88–9, 95–6
assessment. *See specific assessments*
attachment theory 66, 117, 124–5
   adult attachment model 119
   case study 124–5
   between child and caregivers 109–11
   positive attachment 114
   research 118–19, 135
   styles 110–11, 118

attributional beliefs 55
autonomy, workplace 51

Baines, E. 78
Bakhtin, M. M. 31
Bandura, A. 26, 56, 132
Beauchamp, C. 45
behavioural psychological theory 24
beliefs 20, 47, 69–70
   attributional 55
   effort-based 70
   self-efficacy 26, 37, 56, 117, 123
   and values 27, 56, 83, 89, 94, 96, 98–9, 103, 105, 122
Beltman, S. 116, 123
Binet, A. 131
biosocial models 113–17, 136. *See also specific models*
Blatchford, P. 69, 71, 78
Bloom, B. 132
bloomers group (pupils) 67
Bolton, G. 122
Bowlby, J. 66, 109
Boyle, J. 112
Bridge Child Care Consultancy 98
Brooke, G. E. 20
Brookfield, S. 121
Bruner, J. 132

Cameron, R. J. 8, 88
Celik, S. 3
Case studies
   on coaching 9, 12
   constructing teachers' professional identities 35–6
   conversation between NQT and LSA 84–7
   handling stress and burnout 52–4

job descriptions of teacher 21
teacher classroom behaviour management style 124–5
teacher's limits on sharing personals 49–50
Cevik, Y. D. 3
Christian Solidarity International 98
classroom environment 51, 61–5
   ability grouping (*see* ability grouping of pupils)
   mixed-age class 62
   seating arrangements 62–3
classroom management 14, 24, 58
   behaviour 10, 25, 89, 124–5
classroom observation 4, 59–62, 72
classroom teacher(s) 13–14, 51, 67
coaching process
   case study 9, 12
   evaluation 12
   relationship 3–7, 11–12
   strategies 10–12
   teacher 8–11
   vs. counselling 13
cognitive psychology 24, 29–31
cognitive theories 112–13
Collaborative Group Work 80
collaborative learning 74–8
communication. *See* effective communication skills
competent teacher(s) 2, 32, 98
Continuing Professional Development (CPD) 14, 26
cooperative learning 74–8
counselling 12–13, 15, 48
critical/negative feedback 4
Croll, P. 89
curriculum 23–4, 26, 63–5, 69–70, 107, 130, 137

Darling-Hammond. L. 2
Day, C. 54
decision structuring dialogue (DSD) 105–6
deductive assessment 24
DeMauro, A. 44
depersonalization 31
developmental cascades model 114
developmental tasks approach 115

Dewey, J. 5, 120, 130–1
   aspects of reflective thinking 4
diathesis-stress model 114, 136
dis-equilibrium 5
double-loop learning 95, 97–8, 101
dropout 43, 133

education
   educational and developmental psychology 15
   educational progress of pupil 69–70
   primary 131
   psychology in 130–2
   technology in 135–6
Education Resource Information Centre (ERIC) 21
educators, implications for 57–8
effective communication skills 83, 103, 135–6
   Accessible Dialogue (*see* Accessible Dialogue framework)
   communication strategies 96
      Model I communication strategies 89, 99, 101, 104
      Model II/Critical Dialogue strategies 88–91
   developing 88–9, 94
   Guiding Principles 89, 96, 99, 105
   problem-solving 89, 92, 94, 101–2, 105–6, 135
   Theories of Action (*see* Theories of Action)
   through social media 135–6
effective teacher/teaching 2, 37, 56, 133
   elements of 24
effort-based beliefs 70
elementary teachers 89, 118–19
emotions 32, 43–4, 47, 109, 133
   emotional bond 66
   emotional experience 118–19
   emotional intelligence 25–6, 35, 37, 116
   emotion-focused coping strategy 112, 117
   negative 52, 134
   positive 116
   social-emotional development 2, 109
end-of-year assessment 123
Espoused Theories of Action *vs.* Theories in Use 95–7

Index

eudaimonic perspective of well-being 44, 134
expectations of teachers 21, 24, 30–2, 34, 37, 39–40, 47, 65
   and academic progress of pupil 69–70
   effects 67–8, 70 (*see also specific effects*)
   implications for classroom practice 70
   research 69
experienced teacher(s) 2, 32, 38, 118–20, 132
Experience in Close Relationships (ECR) questionnaire 118

Facebook 135
feedback 5, 12, 14, 88, 93, 96, 102, 104, 117, 132
   critical friend 3
   critical/negative 4
   good 24
   high-quality 4
   importance of 2–3
   peer 3
   positive 106
Feucht, F. C. 122
figured worlds theory 29, 31–2
Folkman, S. 112
formative assessment 14, 24
formative learning process 129
Fullan, M. 23, 26–7

Gagné, R. 132
gene–environment interaction effects 114
Glenn, W. J. 4
group identity 19
group membership 30
   in-group 30, 32
   out-group 31
GROWER model 6–8
Gulliford, A. 24
Gu, Q. 54

Hämäläinen, R. P. 105
hard skills 47
Hartup, W. W. 74
Haslaman, T. 3
hedonic perspective of well-being 44, 133
heterogeneous ability grouping 63–4
Hibbert, P. 122

Holland, D. 31
home-based factor 89
homogenous ability grouping 65
Hunter, S. 112

indirect chain effects 113
individual accountability 76
inductive assessment 24
in-group membership 30, 32
institutional-specific skills 98
interaction(s) 76, 80, 85–8, 94, 104, 114, 117, 123, 137. *See specific interactions*
   classroom 111
   gene–environment 114
   group 77
   one-to-one 61
   peer relations and 72–4, 134
   professional 135
   pupil–pupil 71
   social 61, 65–8
   teacher–pupil 61, 65–72, 134–5
inter-group relations 30, 46
Internal Working Models (IWMs) 109–11, 117, 126
International Teacher Professional Identity Survey 36
interventions 5, 44, 109, 114, 125, 134
intragroup relations 30
IRF Sequence, interaction pattern 72
Iwanicki, E. F. 48

Jacobson, L., *Pygmalion in the Classroom* study 67
James, W. 131
   Talks to teachers and to students on some of life's ideals 130
Jennings, P. 44
job satisfaction 19, 39, 44, 116, 123, 132, 134, 136–7
Johnson, D. W. 77
Johnson, F. 77

Kolb, D., learning process 120–1
Koomen, H. M. Y. 37, 123
Kutnick, P. 78
Kyriacou, C. 52

language 19, 27, 31, 72
Langworthy, M. 23
Larrivee, B. 120
Lazarus, R. S. 112
Learning Conversations model 88
learning process 70, 126, 131
    cooperative/collaborative 74–8
    double-loop 95, 97–8, 101
    effective pupil 107
    experiential 132
    formative 129
    interactions 61–2
    Kolb's model of 120
    passive 71
    single-loop 95, 97–8
Learning Support Assistant (LSA), NQT and 84–7
lesson study process 13
Lichtenberg, J. W. 95
line management supervision 3, 10–11
Lortie, D. C. 20

magical thinking 97
Main, M. 110
Masten, A. S. 115
mediators 114, 119
mental health 2, 15, 43–4, 52, 113–14. *See also* well-being
    resilience and 54–5, 108
mental hygiene movement 109
Miller, A. 24
Miller, G. 131
mixed-ability grouping 64
Model I Communication Strategies 89
Model II/Critical Dialogue communication strategies 88–91
moderators 114
modes of reflexivity 122
Monsen, J. J. 8, 88
Montessori, M. 132
Moses, D. 89

Neisser, U. 131
newly qualified teacher (NQT), LSA and 84–7
New South Wales *Code of Conduct* (2014) 49–50

Nuthall, G. 61

Oldfield, J. 116
organizational dimensions 44–5
out-group membership 31

passive learning 71
pedagogical reflection 120
peer co-learning approaches 74–7
peer feedback 3
perfectionism 58
personal attributes 116
personal identity (self) 19, 31, 37, 39, 46
person-focused biosocial model 113
physical context of classroom 61, 77
Piagetian theory 120
Piaget, J. 5, 75, 131
positive psychology 116, 136
positive adaptation of child 113, 115
practice supervision 2–3, 51
preschool teacher 20
pre-service training/teachers 34, 122
primary appraisal process 112. *See also* secondary appraisal process
primary caregivers 109–10
primary education in France 131
primary school teachers 78, 89
probationary periods 51
problem-focused coping strategy 112
problem-solving process 5–6, 89, 92, 94, 101–2, 105–6
professional accountability model 26
professional artistry of teaching 120
professional development 2, 17, 22, 45, 136–7
professional identity. *See* teacher professional identity
professional learning 2, 5, 36
Professional Learning Community (PLC) 13–14
progressive education movement 131
protective factors 108, 113–17
psychodynamic theory 24
psychological theory 25, 29–33, 107, 109
psychology in education 130–2, 137
psychosocial dimensions 45

pupil–pupil interactions 71

Radford, J. 71
reflection 3, 119–20, 124
    case study 124–5
    and coaching relationship 3–7
    critical 120–1, 129
    learnings 122–3
    pedagogical 120
    reflection-for-action 121, 132
    reflection-in-action 5, 120
    reflection-on-action 5, 120
    and reflective practice 120–1, 129
    and reflexivity 121–2, 124–5, 132–3
    thoughts and 10
    triad reflection model 121
reflective practitioner 2, 129
reflective thinking 4, 8
regrouping pupils 64
research 2, 31
    effective communication 105–6
    improving effectiveness of group work in schools (*see* SPRinG project)
    psychological well-being 44
    SMILE model 13–14
    social identity theory 46
    student-teacher attachment 118–19
    on teacher professional identity 33–7
    teacher–pupil relationships 66
    'Validity and reliability of questionnaire on perceived professional identity among teachers (QIPPE) scores' 38–9
resilience. *See* teacher resilience
resilient teachers 54–5
Riley, P. 118
Robinson, V. 88, 102
Rogers, C. 48, 120
Rogers, C. R. 19
role conflict 47–8
role identity theory 29–30, 32
role-play with colleague 103–4
Rolfe, G. 121
Rosenthal, R., *Pygmalion in the Classroom* study 67
Rutter, M. 113, 115

Sammons, P. 123
Saxton, E. A. 112
Schön, D. A. 5, 88–9, 95–6, 120
school climate 56
school-related factor 89
Schwab, R. L. 48
scientist-practitioner role 2, 5
secondary appraisal process 112. *See also* primary appraisal process
secondary school teachers 78
self-determination theory 29
self-efficacy. *See* teacher self-efficacy
self-esteem 25, 30–1, 52
self-fulfilling prophecies effect 68, 70
self-reflection 2–3, 116, 123, 136
self-regulation 24, 30, 115, 117, 122, 135
self-verification 29–30
semantic approach 22
setting, ability grouping 64
Shared Mentoring in Learning Environments (SMILE) programme 13–14
Simon, T. 131
single-loop learning 95, 97–8
Skinner, B. F. 132
Skinner, E. A. 112
Slotte, S. 105
smile rotation process 14
social cognitive theory 56
social comparison process 30, 46
social context of classroom 61, 71, 77, 132, 137
social group 45–7. *See also* teacher(s)
social identity theory 29–32, 45–7, 133
    research 46
social media 43, 135–6. *See also specific companies*
social status 30–1, 70, 74
soft skills 47
Solomon, J. 110
SPRinG (Social Pedagogic Research into Groupwork) project 61, 78–80
Sroufe, L. A. 115
streaming, ability grouping 64
stress 44, 48, 51–4, 108–14, 123, 133–4
    academic 112–13

stress buffering 113
stress reduction techniques 57
student teachers 13–14, 32, 118
summative assessment 24
Summers, J. J. 123
surveys 33–6, 108, 116
sustaining effect 68

Tajfel, H. E. 31, 46
talk theories 96
teacher(s). *See also* social group; *specific teachers*
   challenges 43, 48, 55, 57
   excerpt from interview 60
   expectations (*see* expectations of teachers)
   implications for 40, 105, 126
   new 43, 47, 51, 54, 56, 58, 132, 135, 137 (*see also* newly qualified teacher (NQT))
   roles and responsibilities 20–9, 47–8, 136
      administration 28
      citizenship and ethos 27–8
      communication 27
      development and professional training 26
      pastoral role 25
      role of teaching 22–3
      thematic analysis of job description 21–2, 28
      working with colleagues 26–7
teacher education 20, 34, 45, 131
teacher professional identity 19–20, 26–7, 29–30, 32, 34, 37–40, 47, 56, 123, 133
   constructing (case study) 35–6
   figured worlds theory 31–2
   research 33–7
   role identity theory 29–30, 32
   social identity theory 30–2, 45
teacher–pupil interactions 61, 65–9, 71–2, 134–5
   IRF Sequence 72
   peer co-learning approaches 74–8
   peer relations 72–4
teacher–pupil relationships 37, 48–9, 61, 123, 134–5

closeness 66
conflict 66–7
dependency 66–7
teacher-related factor 89
teacher resilience 54–7, 107–9, 111, 115–16, 122, 136
   learnings 117–18
   and positive psychology 116
   and protective factors 113–16
   three Rs (Reading, Writing and Rithmetic) 107, 123–4, 136
   and transactional coping theory 112–13
teacher self-efficacy 26, 30, 37, 44–5, 56, 108, 123
Teaching and Learning Research Programme 78
teaching assistants 62–3, 65, 67
   interactions between pupils and 71–2
technology in education 135–6
Theories of Action 94, 102
   Espoused Theories *vs.* Theories in Use 95–7
Thomas, L. 45
Thorndike, E. 131
tracking, ability grouping 64
transactional coping theory 112–13
triad reflection model 121
twenty-first-century skills 75, 107
Twitter 135

Understand Society dataset 51
United Kingdom National Foundation for Educational Research 43

'Validity and reliability of questionnaire on perceived professional identity among teachers (QIPPE) scores' study 38–9
variable-focused biosocial model 113
verbal behaviour 83, 89, 98, 103–4, 135
Vygotsky, L. 75, 132
Vygotsky, L. S. 31

walk theories 96
Webb, N. M. 77
Webster, R. 71

Weinstein, R. S. 70
well-being 2, 15, 19, 25, 27, 37, 43–5, 56, 123, 133–4. *See also* mental health
    eudaimonic perspective of 44, 134
    hedonic perspective of 44, 133
    psychological well-being, research 44
    stress and burnout 44, 48, 51–4, 57, 108–14, 123, 133–4
    work and 43–5
WhatsApp groups, education 136
Wheatley, D. 51
whole-class activities/teaching 61, 63, 65, 71
Winkler, A. 122

within-child factor 89
within-class ability grouping 64–5
Woolfolk Hoy, A. 26
Woolfson, L. M. 56
work–life balance 36, 57
workplace autonomy 51
World Health Organization, definition of health 43
Wundt, W. 130–1

Zajac, R. J. 74
Zee, M. 37, 123